DEAL WITH IT, DOLL!

Coaching Yourself Through Crisis

Maribeth,
you're a Doll!
Thank you!
—Christine
2/14/22

BY CHRISTINE O'BRIEN HORSTMAN

Published by the Unapologetic Voice House
www.theunapologeticvoicehouse.com
Scottsdale, AZ.

Cover designer: Heather Brown with Cultural Sponge
Edited by: Maggie Mills

Identifiers:
Paperback ISBN: 978-1-955090-22-3
E-book ISBN: 978-1-955090-23-0

Library of Congress Control Number: 2021922132

For everyone who has ever struggled.

And for Doug.

For being by my side through all of my struggles and triumphs, no matter what.

For better, for worse, in sickness and in health. Well, mostly in sickness.

Thank you for your love, support, and belief in me.

We all have an unsuspected reserve of strength inside that emerges when life puts us to the test.

— Isabel Allende

Contents

Preface

LIFE IS UNPREDICTABLE

When I was a little girl, I often watched soap operas with my mom while she folded laundry or ironed. *Days of our Lives, As the World Turns, One Life to Live.* I can still remember my mom crying during the wedding scenes, laughing at the funny parts, or rolling her eyes when a scene was over the top. My husband remembers his mom calling them her "stories" because that's what they were. They were stories about the big and small dramas of life–some relatable, others (let's be honest, most) beyond ridiculous. Like the whole world is shut in their houses for a pandemic and everyone has to wear masks. Oh, wait.

It's hard to believe what we've been living through, but the producers were on to something that resonated when they were naming these shows. We have one life to live, and the world keeps turning even if all the days of our lives are starting to feel like Groundhog Day. 2020 gave even the most outlandish soap a run for its money, and now years and months later, we still don't know where the plot line's going.

And like my husband and me with our moms, our kids have been watching with us. Watching us watch the shitshow and seeing how we react. We have the most awesome (in the truest sense of the word) of opportunities to show our children how we cope with what's happening in the world at large and in our own homes. Are we calm and collected, or do we have a temper tantrum? Do we support our neighbors like the good people of Salem, or are we wrapped up in our own drama like Erica Kane?

The reality is that life can feel like a complicated, unbelievable soap opera at times, but we get to write our own characters, and we can change the trajectory of the storylines. We can make the trials and tribulations more difficult, or we can see them as an exciting plot twist—a chance to expand our range.

Thankfully, TV has expanded well beyond soap operas to keep us company while we go about our days at home. And in many ways, we are living through the best time in the history of the world to experience a global pandemic with the internet, Facetime, Zoom, and shows on demand.

Still, early on, it was painfully obvious how hard being stuck at home was for almost everyone I talked to. Not just *The Young and The Restless.* (Sorry, not sorry.) But seriously, by a week or so into the pandemic, it seemed like everyone I knew was struggling with feeling bored and antsy and missing social interactions. They kept asking how I was doing in that conspirator's voice. But I was fine. For me, it just didn't feel like life was upside down. Yes, I was stressed and anxious about COVID-19, but I work from home and live with multiple chronic illnesses, so I was very used to being alone at home. In fact, for years, I struggled with feeling lonely and isolated by my health issues. But 15 years of living with chronic illness has made me something of a pro at social distancing.

Having everyone at home was kind of fun. It reminded me of when my son was little and we had a lot of time together during the day. I liked having other people around—hearing my son laughing in his room, sharing lunch with my husband, and having time for puzzles.

Don't get me wrong. I understand why it was hard for so many. But for me, it was just more of the same in many ways. Honestly, most weeks weren't that different than so many weeks I'd had before. But in all these conversations with friends, I realized that I had such a different perspective because of all I had been through. I already knew the mental and emotional resilience required to shelter in place. I knew what it was like being forced to stop and slow down when that wasn't what you wanted to do.

It wasn't an easy journey over the years, but I felt better equipped for our "new normal." I knew that this was truly a question of mind over matter—making the most of what was going right, coupled with a whole lot of self-care.

As a coach and a friend, I found myself sharing something I had always said when talking about my health. "There's nothing like a health crisis to bottom-line things."

When I found out I had cancer, it was like someone had slammed on the brakes. I had already been juggling a baby with working and volunteering, and becoming a working mother had been a big adjustment despite great support from my co-workers and family. I knew with all certainty that working while going through treatment was not realistic for me. I had to concentrate on myself and my family until I was better.

Clarity can be the gift of crisis. I learned to ask what's most important. Being well for my baby was essential. Each day, when I had not a drop of energy left, I had to ask myself what the one big thing I needed to do that day was. Over and over, again and again, in various ways, I had to ask myself, "What's essential?" And that's the exact word we have been using in these unprecedented times, "essential." Essential workers. Essential reasons to leave the house. Essential. How many of us are living life in alignment with what is truly essential?

And then there's the more complicated question of what's seemingly not essential to our survival but critical to our well-being. What have we been taking for granted? What is *really* essential to each of us? Is that the same for our family and friends? Are the things we have prioritized and the life we have created actually in alignment with our core values— with our needs or with our vision for our best life? And maybe that is the question that has caused so much restlessness, the question of what makes you feel like you are just surviving versus really living?

For many, shelter-in-place allowed us to reassess. Time away from the office offered new insights. "I hate commuting." "I had no boundaries between work and home. Now I have more time for family and friends." "I have to leave this job. They don't value me—my ideas are being ignored." "What I really want to do is be a consultant. Maybe I should try that instead of looking for a new job." "I'm putting my job search on hold to publish my book." "I can afford to not work until the new year. With my kids home all summer and my father-in-law sick, I need to just focus on home." These are all actual statements from my clients.

Coupled with what's essential is the question of purpose. Clients and friends are not just asking themselves what their purpose is in terms of work, but also how they are showing up on purpose. And how do we do that when we feel so limited by outside forces? When life throws us a curveball? When the writers of this soap opera called life seem to have gone off the rails?

This was a question I asked myself over and over throughout my health journey. But I didn't go around asking myself, "What's my purpose?" I questioned, "Who am I if I can't work anymore?" I silently condemned myself for bringing nothing to the table if I was no longer earning but the one at home, spending. I felt like an imposter when I stepped back into leadership roles after years of not working or taking jobs that were below my previous levels of experience and responsibility.

I tried being a stay-at-home mom. I worked part-time. I tried to go back full-time. I leaned into volunteer opportunities. At each turn, at some point, I hit a new roadblock that made me wonder why God had given me this personality and this body that seemed forever mismatched. Sometimes, I took it in stride. At other times, I felt overwhelmed and lost. I got tired of trying to reinvent myself when the deck seemed stacked against me. Through it all, I tried to remain positive. I'm naturally wired as an optimist and have always believed in a growth mindset, but I did at times struggle. Big time.

A health crisis can feel like a loss of self on so many levels. You often don't feel like your old self. Sometimes you don't look like your old self. Pain and other factors may cause you to no longer even act like yourself. COVID long-haulers (those who haven't recovered from symptoms after weeks or months) are just the latest to experience this difficult journey.

Job loss can have a similar impact. So much of our identity is tied to work. What's the first thing people ask you when they meet you? "So, what do you do?" Whether you have lost your job, left to stay home as a parent or caregiver, or are too sick to work, it feels strange to have no work identity.

Ours is an achievement-oriented culture. We may have joked about washing our daytime pajamas or wearing hard pants again, but when "I showered today" feels like an accomplishment as a new mom or chronic illness warrior, it can be easy to tell yourself that you are a hot mess. And not in a funny, cute way, but in that mean, ugly voice that we so often reserve for reproaching ourselves.

When you are no longer sure what label fits you, it can create a secondary crisis. When I had thyroid cancer, I swear I went through what could only be described as an existential crisis. This is the scene in the daytime drama where you shut the door, put your back to it, and crumple to the floor. I knew I wasn't going to die from thyroid cancer, but for the first time, the possibility of death seemed tangible. *What had I made of my life? What would my son's life be? How was all this possible at 35?*

After surgery to completely remove my thyroid, I received the final pathology report. My near 100% chance of survival had dropped to close to 80%. It's a great stat for many cancers, but this was going in the wrong direction!

For two months, each day I slipped deeper into exhaustion and struggled to function as my body suffered through the effects of having no thyroid hormones. As I waited for my radioactive iodine treatment, I struggled to process what was happening to me. My mind was fuzzy and slow. The severe shock my body was going through triggered anxiety and depression. For the first time in my life, I questioned: *what if this is all there is?*

The goal was for my body to be so desperate to make those hormones that it would absorb all the radioactive iodine, thereby killing the remaining cancer cells. I cannot even describe to you what it was like because chances are you really can't imagine it. I've now experienced just about every type of tired I think there is—new mom exhaustion, hypothyroid triggered insomnia, fibromyalgia brain fog, rheumatoid arthritis flare fatigue, potassium crash, anemia. You name it, and the thyroid hormone withdrawal was by far the hardest. My body was shutting down. I literally could not keep my eyes open, and at times I couldn't even lift my arm to drink a glass of water. My son would cry for me, and I would be a lump in the chair listening to others console him.

To say it felt bad is an understatement. Who was I if I couldn't care for my own child? These are the hard questions crises cause us to ask. Rationally, with the distance of time or from the perspective of an outside observer, it's an unnecessary and unfair question. But crisis makes a critic of even the most optimistic of us.

We've heard the calls for empathy. Empathetic leadership. Empathy in the hiring process. These are trending topics on LinkedIn. Emergencies and hard times call for empathy. Coping during a crisis requires empathy. Our world, we realize, already needed much more of it. And while the very definition of empathy—"the ability to understand and share the feelings of others"[1]—is to put ourselves in someone else's shoes, we ought to reserve some of that compassion for ourselves. It's one of the lessons I've learned. To be kinder to myself. I still sometimes miss the mark. It's not second nature by any stretch. But thankfully, my husband will tell me when I'm being too hard on myself.

The forced shutdown made many of us realize just how hard it is to slow down, to not have our usual go-to outlets and distractions. What unkind questions does crisis whisper in the quiet to you? Is the voice kind and empathetic? Or does it say things like, "You didn't do enough today. You'll never find another job. You are the worst parent. You look awful. You should be exercising! You should have. You didn't. You'll never." Or the unrelenting, "What if?"

Self-judgment. Self-doubt. They're the creepers in crisis. Rubbing up on you, harshing your vibe. Just when you think you've shaken them off, there they are again. You can and should try killing them with kindness, but chances are you are going to need a few more strategies. They don't easily take "no" for an answer.

What has made the global pandemic so profound is that even when the world stops, the world doesn't stop. And those of us who have dealt with crises before know that this is only too true. People still get cancer. People still die. Babies, thank heavens, are still being born. And the problems in our lives, on the regular, are still challenging. Our kids still won't clean their rooms. Teenagers are still moody. Our relationships are still on the rocks. Our moms are still annoying. (Not you, Mom. That was just an example.) We still want to swipe right and finally meet someone great. As The World Turns, so are the Days of Our Lives.

Life. Keeps. Going. And it is unpredictable. With our clever "2020 vision" slogans at the start of the New Year, we could not have imagined that we would get a collective punch to the gut come spring. You may be going along swimmingly in life and, out of nowhere, face your own crisis. You may have already had more challenges than seem fair for one person to endure. Whether you are still trying to process the pandemic or dealing with a crisis of your own creation, I hope that this book will leave you feeling less alone and so much stronger.

It is also my hope, of course, that you will read the book cover to cover, but you might want to skip ahead to the chapter that is most reflective of where you are struggling. Each chapter, however, is written with lessons in mind that we can all learn from, even if it is not our current challenge. The book is divided between personal change and crisis and professional change and crisis, but we know that a major setback in one area will naturally impact the other.

Our collective health crisis inspired this book, but it's built for the most common curveballs. The stuff many of us face personally and professionally in any given year. The changes most of us will deal with in our lifetimes. What should we do with our lives? How do we handle failure? How do we support our loved ones when they are struggling? All of it.

I started this book at the beginning of the pandemic, and we're still wondering what lies ahead. We never really know, do we? Coping with chronic illness has equipped me with a toolbox to keep going even when my body makes it hard. When I caught COVID during the writing of this book and ended up sick for months, I had to dig deep into that toolbox to cope. I want to help you build your own toolbox for when life makes it hard for you, for when you are no longer sure what lies ahead but have to keep going.

One of the most important tools we have at our constant disposal is our mind. Using positive and affirming language can rewire our brains. We all love free resources, and we should learn to make the most of the free and most powerful resource we have. So, with that in mind (see what I did), at the end of every chapter are mantras to help you manage your mindset.

As a professional coach, I can tell you that the premise behind coaching is not to fix things for you but to lead you to the answer that is already within you. Coaches do this through the process of powerful questioning. You will find a series of powerful questions at the end of each chapter to help you prevent or push through a crisis and cope with change. These questions will help you pull meaning from the lessons learned without having to have lived it yourself. You'll see what I mean when you get there.

Here's to our well-being this year and every year, no matter what unexpected twists and turns life takes. Here's to *The Bold and The Beautiful*. To each one of you building your resilience, facing the hard stuff, and dealing with whatever comes your way.

Part One

PERSONAL

Chapter 1

HEALTH
YOU ARE NOT UNRELIABLE,
YOUR HEALTH IS

YOU ARE NOT UNRELIABLE, YOUR HEALTH IS. IF THIS RESO-nates with you, then you've had yourself a health crisis or two like me, or you are currently living with chronic illness. Or maybe you're living with or know someone who struggles with their health condition, and you get it.

If this doesn't make sense—or you question this state-ment—then thank your lucky stars. It's easy to believe that it won't ever happen to you. More than likely, it's just a mat-ter of time. The countless number of people now suffering from long-haul COVID[2] have been hit hard with this truth. Pre-pandemic, six in ten adults in the United States already suffered from a chronic illness[3], and one in two people will develop cancer[4] in their lifetime. That means if you haven't experienced a health crisis yet, you likely will. Add caregiving into the mix, and you realize not many of us will escape the impact of chronic illness.

While my cancer diagnosis is what turned my life upside down, my complicated health journey started a decade before that. In my twenties, I had a car accident that landed me in the ICU. Through the course of treating me, doctors uncovered issues with my kidney and pain syndromes that were complicated by the accident. That was when I discovered things that I had long thought were normal to live with, were not.

No wonder I was so easily tired and had joked that my insides felt broken after a night of partying in college. It turns out that no one else's side ached with a deep pain after drinking alcohol. That was my deformed kidney!

The periods that one month would be normal and then, the next, would keep me in bed for two days or writhing on the bathroom floor praying I would pass out before vomiting? Endometriosis.

Allergies, exhaustion, and what had been diagnosed as chronic allergic tension fatigue syndrome in high school, were now being classified as chronic fatigue syndrome, what is today typically referred to as myalgic encephalomyelitis or ME/CFS.

The car accident, and the damage and bruising to my abdomen triggered these not so latent conditions that I had been resigned to living with. I had never thought they were as serious as they were. My uterus was thickened to at least twice its normal size, and my pelvic floor was so covered in adhesions that I was warned at 23 to hurry up and have a baby because I needed a hysterectomy. (Spoiler alert—I didn't have a baby until I was 33 and thankfully made it an additional decade before my hysterectomy at 43.)

It's hard to explain the combination of shock and relief you feel when you get a diagnosis for something that has been overlooked, minimized, or misdiagnosed. It's a relief to know it wasn't all in your head. That you're not just anxious or high maintenance. That it's real! That you were right. That what you felt wasn't normal. But it's also scary and overwhelming, and many doctors leave out a considerable amount of critical and helpful information.

I spent hours combing through the Dallas Public Library database searching for articles and information. Yes. That's how old I am, Doll—I couldn't just Google it! I bounced from specialist to specialist and was prescribed numerous pain pills and muscle relaxants concurrently by at least three different doctors that it's a wonder I didn't end up addicted.

The car accident kicked off seven years of pain and infections that I just couldn't seem to beat. I had many great doctors and one or two horrible ones. But after a while, even the good doctors shook their heads and were at a loss to help me. I don't know if people realize that for many of us with multiple chronic illnesses, this is all too common.

I finally came across a book called *How to Save Your Own Life* by Marie Savard, M.D., which gave me the best advice that I still pass on to this day: get copies of all your medical records, including doctor's notes, correspondence between doctors, and complete lab reports. I know what you're thinking. "I have access to everything online now." You don't. What I learned is that there are errors in your chart. There are things doctors have never mentioned to you in your chart. There are assumptions based on your appearance and behavior in your chart. And there is information no one else is putting together in your chart that just might save your own life. That's not the same as the information you have access to in your portal.

Send a formal, written request asking for each of these items. It may cost you a fee, but it will pay off.

In reviewing all my records, I discovered a pattern of abnormal labs that went along with the inflammation of endometriosis but also pointed to an infection that had never been treated that had been showing up year after year. Frustrated by conventional medicine, I searched for a new perspective and went to see an osteopath who had other holistic doctors and practitioners in her practice. I plopped down seven years of lab reports and shared my theories. She listened. She treated me. And I worked with them to rebuild my system after all the antibiotics, anti-inflammatories, and other medications.

The biggest lesson I learned from that chapter in my health journey was that I had to take control. I had to learn as much as possible, and I couldn't assume that the experts always knew best. I could educate myself, and *I* was the expert on my own body and my health history.

I'm not saying I didn't trust my doctors. Nor am I saying I gave up on Western medicine. In fact, I went through a very extreme experimental treatment for my endometriosis, and it worked. I also had the first laparoscopy my OB/Gyn at the time had ever performed. He was young, new, caring, and kind, and I trusted him completely. For years, an image of my uterus sat framed on his shelf. I kid you not. He was so proud of that surgery and liked to show off my wreck of an organ. But over time, we hit an impasse. He'd done all he could. It was a fresh perspective and my detective work pouring over my medical records from every doctor I had ever seen that helped me to take the next step in my healing.

What I learned very clearly in becoming my own health advocate is that at the end of the day, it always comes down to you. No one, and I mean no one, will ever be more motivated than you are to solve your problems. Read that again, Doll, because it's the harsh and empowering truth.

No one, and I mean no one, will ever be more motivated than you are to solve your own problems.

Not even your mom. Not even your dear old dad. You will hit a point in your adult life (sometimes sooner, which is really rough) that you realize your mama and daddy have their own problems and other things to worry about and may lack the time, resources, knowledge, or wherewithal to fix it for you. It is up to you. And that's why adulting is so damn hard.

But I'm here to tell you that it's the only way, and everything you tackle now will help you with everything you tackle later. The more you do, the more you can do. You have no idea how the skills you are building today will equip you for what is in store tomorrow.

For me, and many of you, when our bodies let us down and fail, it breaks us down and cracks us open in raw and powerful ways. Facing the fact that we are physically weak—that we cannot do it all, be it all anymore—makes us so much stronger emotionally. And a heck of a lot wiser.

But that shift does not happen overnight. With the loss of health typically comes the loss of productivity, and with that comes the loss of identity.

Who am I if I can't work? Who am I if I can't compete? Who am I if I can't parent?

With the loss of health often comes a loss of self because your body doesn't work like it once used to or look like it once did. Your hair might be falling out, and your clothes falling off your frame. Or maybe you are packing on the pounds between your new meds and your inability to exercise—let alone get out of bed. You don't look like yourself. You don't feel like yourself. It can get depressing. Which can make getting out of bed that much harder.

When you can't keep up, you often end up dropping out. Your friends and family, no matter how supportive, have their own lives to lead. And they are. Which can leave you feeling like you are stuck on the sidelines.

Hobbies you once enjoyed may now be too taxing or too challenging. At its worst, rheumatoid arthritis in my hands made doing almost any task for too long difficult. Before, journaling always helped when I was feeling down. And then it would hurt to write or type. I loved adult coloring books, they took my mind off things and made me feel creative. Then it hurt to color. *I should bake some cookies*, I would think. Then I would find that I had no arm strength or hand grip to hold the spoon. You get the picture.

It can be challenging to lift yourself up when the old ways don't work. It can also be a strain on relationships. (More on that in Chapter 3!)

While, on the one hand, a health crisis can feel extremely limiting, it can also be incredibly freeing. As I said at the start of this book, there's nothing like a health crisis to bottom-line things. You get down to what's essential, what matters most to you. For me, that was having the energy to be present as a mom.

My son was an 18-month-old when I was diagnosed with thyroid cancer, and I was struggling with extreme fatigue and insomnia. I came to a crossroads when it was time to determine if and when I could return to work. When I looked at what I valued most, the choices before me became easier to make. When it came down to determining how to juggle my treatment with parenting and work, I knew it didn't make sense for me to try. I chose to say "no" to work. It was a financial sacrifice but when I admitted I couldn't do it all, the choice of what I then wanted to do with the energy I had was obvious.

Once I stopped working, I knew I had to lighten my load a little more. At a minimum, I had five months of treatment on the horizon. I had been running my college alumni group for ten years at that point. I had wanted to let go, but there always seemed a good reason to keep going, and, in the previous two years, I had been talked back into it when I wanted to move on. It was amazing how quickly someone accepted me saying, "no" when I told them I had cancer. That was an interesting lesson in and of itself.

How many times had I said, "yes" when I wanted to say, "no"? How many times had I gone against my gut? How many times had I let others, and even myself, talk me into something? How often had I been hanging on to things that had run their course?

For years I had been "burning the candle on both ends," as my mother would say. There were always signs that my body couldn't handle it. I wish I had listened better back then. At first, it was because I was young, and didn't want to miss out. Then, I became a working mom who wanted to be successful in all areas of life. I wanted to accomplish a lot. I remember how hard I tried to keep up with everything and everyone when my son was a baby. It wasn't realistic when the fact was that I had entered this new phase of life that was demanding and exhausting. But I kept trying.

Finally, when I tried to reach down for that extra energy it wasn't there. The well was dry. That's when I knew something was wrong. But even if my thyroid hadn't been dying, I wonder how depleted the well had already become?

WE ALL HAVE LIMITATIONS

I had been trying to rebuild my health in the years leading up to my pregnancy and had a lot of success with it. I exercised consistently. I ate an anti-inflammatory diet. (Quite possibly with too much soy in it.) But I was still pushing myself past my limits regularly. Having my body slam on the brakes because it was crashing, should have been the ultimate wake-up call, but I still sometimes struggle with finding a balance. A balance of not pushing when I'm tired, of eating with real intention, of refilling and recharging my system in meaningful ways. It has been an uphill battle. I have programmed myself through many years and it's been hard to undo.

I know some of it is my personality. Some of it is my need to be all-in on a project. But I wonder how much of the programming has come from external messages as well. I wonder to what extent our cult of productivity—the "I'll sleep when I'm dead" mentality—contributes to my health challenges? I wonder how it contributes to our collective lack of well-being.

How many times have you had to go to the bathroom, but waited to accomplish just one more thing before getting up from your desk? How many times do you skip a meal because you are going and blowing and just don't have time? And then when you do eat, is it still on the run?

How many coaches have told a player to play through the pain? How many times did you stay up even when your body wanted to shut down? You had to write the paper, meet the deadline, go to the party, or maybe just finish the movie.

Before the pandemic, how often had you sent your kid to school with a fever? How many of you went to work even though you were sick?

Neglecting our physical needs and the messages that our bodies send is a strange way of putting ourselves last, isn't it? We are constantly ignoring our body's hardwiring and messaging system. We tell ourselves I don't really feel that way. I don't need to eat. To eat less. To rest. To sleep. Or to get up and move.

You can imagine that when I first started having signs of rheumatoid arthritis, I talked myself out of them. Yes, I thought it was weird that I kept waking up unable to move my right arm. It would be completely numb. It was weird that my feet and knees and legs hurt badly from the first moment they hit the floor until at least a good hour after waking up. I didn't ignore these strange symptoms completely. At first, I thought some were still tied to my thyroid levels and related problems I had with my calcium levels—a side effect from my thyroidectomy. I even talked to my doctors about it. But I didn't really want to deal with it or pursue exactly what was going on.

I certainly wasn't fighting for answers like I did when I suspected thyroid cancer. I was beyond sick of going to the doctor at this point. I was sick and tired of being sick and tired. I desperately wanted life to be back to normal that I fought through it daily like many of us do until my body simply could not keep fighting through it.

I was out in the backyard gardening when I got the strangest feeling of warning bells. I struggle to put it into words but imagine when you get a full-body chill, a chill that chases through you. It was sort of like that, only accompanied by a charge of adrenaline that something was very wrong. I had been hurting a bit and getting stiff, but I had just one more bed to finish. I picked up the last bag of soil and suddenly, I could barely move my hands. The "chill" shot through my limbs, and it was like all my muscles were shutting down. I dropped everything, went inside to my bedroom, and started undressing. I was filthy, but I knew I needed to get in bed right then. Urgently. I intuitively knew that wherever I landed I was not going to be able to move again, so bed seemed like the best and only place for me to go.

I called my husband, Doug, to say that I wasn't going to be able to pick up our son, Patrick, and I didn't—couldn't—get out of that bed, except with someone helping me inch my way to the bathroom, for three full days.

Once I was able to walk on my own again, I still couldn't get up the stairs. I am not joking or exaggerating when I say I had to crawl up the stairs. I couldn't get my legs to lift high enough to climb them. It was a nightmare. I finally called the rheumatologist my doctor had recommended, and I was diagnosed the same day that I saw him. My blood work and x-rays confirmed all the physical signs and symptoms. I had rheumatoid and psoriatic arthritis with fibromyalgia. Just like my grandmother.

Me of all people—me, who had listened before when my body wasn't working, who fought to be heard and to get a correct diagnosis—chose not to listen to myself, to my body. Why do we do this?

Through all of this, I have learned that if I don't listen to the whispers, eventually, the universe, by way of my body, will hit me over the head with the message. And when that doesn't work, it will find another way to smack me into admission.

The early days of the arthritis/autoimmune diagnoses were extremely hard, but I was determined to claw my way back to having a functioning life. I decided to try a little side hustle with my friend, selling products I had long used and believed in and knew were healthier for people's homes. I also dove into volunteering in the neighborhood and at my son's school because I wanted to embrace this new phase of life now that he was starting school, and hoped to make and build friendships for the both of us.

One afternoon, I was totally stressed out and running around, knowing that I was taking on too much when my health was already inconsistent. I tackled business building and volunteering like I always did, by throwing myself into it. Working in the middle of the night when I had insomnia, thinking I could push through it. I knew deep down that I should cancel the evening's event for the business that my friend and I were building. But I didn't want to admit that it was too much and that I felt overwhelmed. I didn't want to let her or anyone else down. And more than anything, I just wanted to be able to do what I wanted to be able to do.

That evening, I got in the car with my body hurting, my mind preoccupied and my whole self just generally feeling on overload. I started the car and heard a loud bang. I had backed smack into a telephone pole! That was when I finally started listening. And the first voice I heeded was the one telling me I was in no shape for the event that night. So I made the hard call to not attend, and guess what? It was

OK. It was not the world-ending catastrophe I imagined it would be.

How much anxiety and trouble would I have saved—not to mention a deductible—had I really listened to myself the day before?

Getting honest with the fact that we all have limitations has been hard for me. I know it's hard for a lot of you, too. We praise people who work through cancer treatments, who come to work because it's only walking pneumonia, or whatever the case may be. We honor this idea of pushing our limits because, no pain, no gain.

Don't get me wrong, I understand there are times when we need to show that we can go further, fight harder, get it done at all costs. But when that is the default, it can lead to trouble. Especially if you don't replenish, refuel, recover, or recalibrate with care after you've pushed the boundaries.

Many of us get so used to this cycle of stress and adrenaline that we don't know how else to operate. It can be very humbling and hard to accept when our bodies finally force us to slow down or come to a full stop. The price we pay for not listening—from burnout to full-blown illness—can be high. We all have limited time and energy. Too often, it's only when we've gone far past that or taken it for granted, until we can no longer do it anymore, that we realize this absolute truth.

LETTING GO, SO YOU CAN HANG ON

One of the reasons for our resistance is that we like to think we are in control. I hate to tell you, Doll, but we're not. We want to be. Badly. That's why we take comfort in and marvel at the people who work through six months of chemo. While stories like that can be inspiring, it's not realistic for everyone. You can be super positive and the perfect patient and still have negative out-

The antidote to resistance is acceptance.

comes. You can do all the right things for your health and still get sick. We are not in complete control.

The antidote to resistance is acceptance. Accepting a new diagnosis and that we aren't in control of the big picture is one thing but learning to accept it daily and what that really means and looks like is another.

Acceptance isn't always easy. There were times when I would do everything in my power to manage my time and energy, to take good care of myself, and I still would wake up feeling like someone had poured concrete on me. I could rest but it wouldn't necessarily mean I could ward off a flare-up of symptoms. Frankly, I could rest but it wouldn't even mean I would end up feeling rested.

It was incredibly frustrating. I could try to influence func-tioning at my best, but I had to adapt and adjust when that didn't work, which meant accepting where my body's abilities were each day. And so that became a new struggle—acknowledging how I felt without being overwhelmed by it and learning to listen to the messages, the emotional and physical cues, while they were still whispers, rather than full-on screams before I couldn't move or backed into another telephone pole.

This is harder than it sounds when you have some degree of pain every day and pain levels that are not necessarily stable throughout the day. The inconsistent nature of your symptoms is one of the hallmarks of chronic illness. Fatigue is the other thing that makes it hard to know how you "really feel." Fatigue is the constant companion of so many chronic illnesses.

And on days when the pain and fatigue were so bad that I felt like a shadow of myself, I had to dig deep to keep myself going. I had to dig deep to counter the negative thoughts that said, *you will never get back to who you were. You will never be better. Your son has never known the real you—the you before sickness defined you.*

In trying to cope with that feeling that no matter how hard I tried, I couldn't control how I physically felt, I started telling myself *everything is always changing.* I remembered a mantra I had read that stuck with me, it said: "Everything is changing from one moment to the next." I repeated that to myself over and over until I felt less attached to how things were supposed to be. I tried to send love to my body even when I was mad at it. I tried to be thankful for the medical options I had that my grandmother didn't have. I recounted my gratitude for the little things that helped me so much—my heating pad, the bathtub (and that I could still get in and out of it!), Epsom salts, music, candles, flowers, the fresh air coming in through the door to the backyard, my puppy, my home, looking out the window at the trees. I would list the simplest things that brought me joy and reminded me of how fortunate I was in so many ways.

Letting go of what I wanted, what I expected, what I hoped for allowed me to be grateful for what was. That's when I started intentionally thinking about my toolbox. My strategies for coping and living. When you are in a chronically stressful situation, the usual pick-me-ups often stop working.

Sometimes your meds stop working. Sometimes what once brought you comfort, no longer does. You find you have to keep trying new things, going back to old things, coming up with new combinations.

FILLING YOUR TOOLBOX

Over time, I had been developing a toolbox on the medical side. Additional pain meds and muscle relaxants, gels, creams, and patches for the worst days. I added over-the-counter treatments, homeopathic remedies, and Chinese herbs. I had my team of practitioners who helped me, and I tried different types of body and energy work. I went to therapy and even used hypnosis to manage my pain.

All these pieces helped greatly, but in the day-to-day, it was my own arsenal of pick-me-ups that often got me through. Phone calls to family and friends. Walking and stretching, my heating pad and massage mat, lots and lots of baths. Did I mention baths? Sometimes, I took a bath three times a day to manage my pain levels. A mountain of pillows and improvements to my room, so when I had to live in there for stretches of time, I could do so with greater ease and enjoyment.

I also had my go-to time fillers—books, TV, movies, magazines, Pinterest, Facebook. Social media gave me a connection to people when I was often housebound and provided support and information from other chronic illness warriors online. And I was able to help others by sharing my knowledge and journey. Trying new things, going back to old things, adding to my arsenal.

Over time my toolbox became more like Mary Poppins' carpet bag. A mix of real things and a little magical thinking to shake things up. I learned small things could shift the energy—a new pillow, a favorite sweater, moving the chair to a different spot. Sitting in another room for a while. Music, stretching, or aromatherapy. Small shifts in the energy in your environment and your body can keep you from sinking into negativity. I cannot stress how important this is.

At my worst physically and mentally, I learned to stop tormenting myself with all that I couldn't do. I learned to let it go if the dishes or laundry sat for days on end. And I learned to combat my own messed-up mindset. It was so easy to constantly think about what wasn't getting done, how behind I was, how bad it felt to have not accomplished things. I would find myself listing everything I hadn't gotten done that I had hoped to do. I finally had to start using a technique that I still use to this day when the voice inside my head won't stop nagging me; I start to list of everything I have done.

I got up and brushed my teeth. I let the dogs out. I put in a load of laundry. I took a shower. I answered three emails. I made myself a meal. I know this sounds a bit pathetic and crazy, because the bar is so low, but I promise you it is powerful. Sometimes we have to start with the smallest steps to keep moving forward. I had to combat my thoughts to focus on a sense of accomplishment for self-care to feel like a true accomplishment. I had to focus on a positive list.

Like the small shifts in energy, even the smallest shift towards positive thoughts makes an impact. I promise that it works. This technique never fails to calm my anxiety and feelings of failure. It puts me in a place of *I'm still here and I'm not giving up. I have, I can, and I will—one small baby step at a time if I must.* I may not be able to control the fact that I live with chronic illness, or control how I feel each day, but I can

control how it impacts me
mentally and emotionally.

It is mind over matter, not just to get me up and out and still functioning and doing, but mind over matter to keep me from getting down, in a constant state of frustration, dis-

Our bodies are amazing and complex—and full of knowledge.

appointment, and mourning. All these small steps and tools keep me feeling positive and engaged in my life—keep me trying to live and be myself—keep me optimistic.

I remember when I was in natural childbirth class, they told us that at some point during labor we would want to give up and say, "I can't do this. It's too much. I'm done." They told us that would be the best moment because it was the emotional signpost that we were in transition, that the baby was almost here. And, besides the fact that as we all know there would be no option of giving up, typically the baby would arrive within 45 minutes of that moment.

Of all the points of labor, I remember that one so clearly. I was exhausted. I was on all fours, and I wanted to collapse. My legs ached and felt weak. I wanted it all to stop. I told the midwife that I couldn't continue. It was exactly what she told me I would say. But somewhere underneath the pain and exhaustion, and the worry that I couldn't do it, somewhere underneath my conscious mind, my subconscious and my body knew better, so I kept doing what my body demanded of me and I showed myself that I have an inner strength that had previously gone untested. Deep down, from all the preparation I could tap into, knowing that I had to do this and that even if I felt like I couldn't go on, that I would, and that the sweetest reward would soon be arriving, was so strong.

In childbirth, I had to surrender and go deep inside myself to a different kind of knowing. Our bodies are amazing and complex—and full of knowledge. Our bodies speak to us in so many ways if we commit to listening. We have to listen to the physical warnings as well as the emotional ones. And we have to listen to our instincts. That was the gift of knowing that natural childbirth gave me. I surrendered completely to my instinctual being. Instead of fighting the pain, I let it guide me and tell me when to push and what to do. This required going into myself on such a level that would be hard to replicate. But I have tried.

Hypnosis and meditation have helped me to manage some of my symptoms and allow me to surrender and move through pain rather than resist and intensify it. They have also helped me to tap into reserves of energy, strength, and positive emotions too. Accepting exactly where you are is the only way to move through it and out of it.

YOU CAN DO IT ALL, BUT NOT ALL AT ONCE

Acknowledging that my body no longer worked the way it once did and that it required way more rest meant I had to come to terms with my limitations. I had to accept that I could not manage a full, normal day or workload. That was just reality. Hoping, wishing, or trying did not change it. I had to accept where I was and determine what was now doable. I had to stop focusing on the loss and what I couldn't do and, from my new vantage point, ask myself what was possible. This is what people mean by embracing your new normal.

Accepting that there is no definitive cure, and that remission does not happen for everyone, was the first step. This does not mean that I have ever stopped trying to get better or manage my disease. However, always hoping for a cure that didn't come, was quickly becoming counterproductive, so I had to live my life the best way that I could and not wait until things were better. I had to live in the present.

One of the ways I first came to terms with my limitations was by realizing that there are seasons in life. That at some point I would get to work again, but being a mom was what was most important now. I tried to embrace this fact and to see the big picture.

When I started telling myself that I could do everything I wanted in life, maybe just not all at once, it took some of the pressure off. I still have had moments of comparison when I see another woman that I know who seems to have it all—the kids, the career, travel, a great body—I get jealous. I think about what I thought it would all look like, but I have to let that pass. I have to remember that I am on my own journey, and it is not a competition or a race. That I may be the turtle, but I will cross the finish line. I will accomplish my goals. And I always remind myself that small wins are still wins.

Now that my son is older, and I have several more seasons under my belt, I realize how accurate this has been. I can do it all, just not all at once. I tell myself the same thing on my bad days when the pain and flu-like feelings are too hard to shake. I tell myself, *do as much as you can, for as long as you can, as best as you can.* I may not be able to clean the whole house in half a day like I used to, but even if I clean one counter, or organize one drawer, it puts me closer to where I want to be. It's one positive, proactive step within what I *can* do. Small wins really and truly add up.

By accepting that I can't do everything all the time, I have been able to continue to embrace the idea that there will be seasons in my life of better health, greater productivity, and times when I have to lay fallow. I have had to trust that when I am held in place, something new will blossom later. So far, I have found that to be true.

My health isn't static, my cells in my body aren't static, life is not static. In some ways it's not my health that has necessarily gotten better, it is the demands in my life that have shifted and evolved which are having a positive impact. Some were deliberate choices; I no longer vacuum, for example. A small but impactful thing. I rarely go grocery shopping. These weekly tasks took too much out of me. I realized I could stay on track with other more beneficial things by eliminating them, so I did. Other shifts were simply time marching on.

Remember my original mantra—everything is changing from one moment to the next? Life has changed and my family has evolved. My son has grown up. The physical demands of being a parent are so different from when I first got diagnosed. That has had a positive impact on me in ways I never considered years ago.

Now my son is driving and half-way through high school, and I see how much time I will have to care for myself and once again lean deeper into my career. If you are feeling limited by your health, by your body, there is such a fear that it will continue to get worse. It might, but other things may also shift that allow you to navigate those changes with greater ease.

KNOW YOUR BOUNDARIES

Another thing that will make accepting your new normal a little easier, is letting go of the fear of disappointing others with what you can no longer do. This is part of the struggle of chronic unrelenting illness. You can feel like you are failing at life. You are not. But when you must cancel plans because you are unwell or have to decline another invitation because you are trying to be honest about your limits, it's hard. It sometimes hurts because not only do you have to manage your own mindset, but you also worry about letting other people down. And it gets exhausting to constantly be measuring, can I? can't I? and should I? Push, pull, push, pull. The more honest you can be about your energy, abilities, and priorities, the easier it will be to set realistic expectations and create healthy boundaries.

You will face moments of resistance from within and from without. Other people in your life will likely struggle with these same issues. They will want to be helpful and supportive but not yet realize that they are trying to hang onto what was and trying to control what could be. They will want you to use your time and energy in ways that make sense to them. What I can pretty much guarantee you is that somewhere along the way, you will also have to accept that the limitation of your illness will upset others. The boundaries and choices you make will likely be criticized.

Sometimes you will hold back when maybe you could have pushed yourself. Many times, you will overdo it no matter how hard you try. Other times you will gladly pay the price because the person, event, or moment was so worth it. Only you can decide. Read that again, Doll. Only you can decide.

And no matter how hard you try; it's still likely things won't go as expected because your body is inconsistent.

There were times when I felt judged as flaky or unreliable, despite my long list of verified diagnoses. I even had people suggest to me, and others, that perhaps I was a hypochondriac, or just being dramatic. I had to keep reminding myself that I am not unreliable, my body is. I had to come to terms with the reality that some people would not accept that. They still operated under a false sense of control and a false sense that medical problems are easily addressed. Many people would rather deny the diagnosis than admit that medical professionals can't cure everything.

And this is the truth about any kind of boundary you set in life. You have to accept it and live with it and anticipate that others often won't like it. That's because their boundary-setting criteria may be quite different from yours, and they may lack the perspective to understand yours.

There were times when I was told that I would probably be healthier if I stopped working—that the stress wasn't good for me. And then I would be told, it would probably be better if I were working, that I was spending too much time thinking about my illness and getting out of the house would be good for me. *By the same person.* I'm telling you, Doll, you cannot win. You have to be OK with your choices. Which honestly, is an important life lesson. It's nice when others understand. You have to be OK if they don't.

I have always been a party girl. I love a late night with friends, talking, laughing, and, once upon a time, dancing. Like most of us, as we have kids and get older, there are fewer late nights than we had in our youth. But they still happen. Are they the best for me? Probably not, physically. A steady sleep schedule is better, but the amount of pain-related insomnia and sleepless nights I experience because I can't get comfortable, or my mind won't shut off far outweighs the nights out dancing or staying up late talking. So, I allow myself the pleasure to be in the moment with my friends. Not everyone appreciates my perspective. I no longer care. I know that what I need emotionally, to feel like me, matters.

Frankly, I could live my life very regimented and still have a flare of my symptoms. Hormone changes, the freaking weather (do not get me started on barometric pressure!)—there are so many factors that play into it. And here's the deal, I am not a restrained, regimented person. It just isn't me and we have to be ourselves.

People with their own unhealthy habits have lectured me on why I should curb some of mine. (Warning, do not try to convince me to stop drinking Sunkist.) Unlike them, I have accepted that I can't control everything, that my symptoms change daily. I get that it's hard for people to wrap their heads around the nature of chronic illness. Sometimes their concerns come from hating to see me struggle and suffer, which is sweet. But some of it comes because they are disappointed when I can't take part in what they want me to do.

I'm not going for perfection. I'm going for management and balance. I'm going for meeting my physical needs as well as my emotional and mental needs. My entire life has been impacted by my chronic illness. I can't let it take my personality, too.

You have to be you, Doll. You have to define yourself. I'm not saying hold on to stupid habits like continuing to smoke when you have heart issues or lung cancer. I'm talking about letting loose and having fun. I'm talking about still gardening, even if your knees ache for days.

Chances are the behavior you are judging someone with chronic illness for continuing, has already been modified. And sometimes we will make the wrong choices. Push when we shouldn't have. Hold back when maybe we could have pulled it off. We'll be punished enough for it both physically and emotionally. We don't need guilt and judgment from others piled on.

And isn't that true of most things in life? Our judgments and desire to fix and manage other people's lives are more often a reflection of our own needs than the other person's.

Acceptance has meant turning off that constant refrain of judgment and concern over what other people will think, and how they will feel, that goes on in my own mind. If people only knew what agony I go through over deciding to go to an event or if I should cancel. It's still torturous to me at times. I finally know I have to stay home once I am in that decision-making loop. Disappointing people and being disappointed myself is still very hard for me. It bums my husband out when I can't go with him to a party or dinner with friends. I have missed out on so much with my son. I have spent holidays in bed while everyone else is gathered at a relative's house or even in my own dining room. It sucks. But it really is what it is and, again, ruminating over it does not change it.

Now my husband pulls the plug when I can't bring myself to make the decision or say the words. For both of us, understanding the emotional warning signs of how I feel has been as important as learning the physical signs.

PUTTING POSITIVE IN PERSPECTIVE

"Go slow, but keep going," is another version of putting the positive in perspective. All of these sayings, affirmations, and mantras are also small steps in the bigger picture of staying positive. I don't mean that I pretend to feel good all the time. I don't. Sometimes, I bitch about it and, sometimes, I hate to admit, I am bitchy because of it. It can be hard to be nice when you are hurting. As I've said, I gave up on a cure long ago, of total remission of my autoimmune issues. I still hope on some level, but I no longer think, "if," "when," "then." I operate on a "This may be the best it ever is, so how do I make the best of it?" basis.

During my cancer experience, there was such a push by the medical professionals for me to be positive. There's some good data to support a positive mindset and good outcomes, but I found that the way it was practiced was often a bit twisted. Rather than give me realistic expectations of the bad parts, they glossed over them. They didn't want me to worry and wanted me to stay positive. But not having accurate expectations made the hard parts harder.

I thought I was supposed to be better quickly from all their positive approaches and when I wasn't, I began to feel like I was letting everyone down. I was so tired of being asked how I was doing with the weight of so much expectancy. I remember being asked by a friend if I could go on a walk and I explained I couldn't go that far, and she responded, "You're that tired?" Yes, I was that tired, many months after my initial treatment. Finally, after one despondent check-up, my surgeon told me it was going to take a good year for me to regain my energy. That would have been helpful to know from the beginning.

Positivity is not being in denial of the hard things we must face. Positivity is not sugar coating a shitty situation. Positivity is acknowledging and facing facts but choosing to believe you can get through whatever is ailing you. Positivity is venting sometimes, but not dwelling on the negative. Positivity is gratitude even when we are sad or disappointed or in pain. Positivity is knowing there will be better tomorrows than the today we may be suffering through. Positivity is the silver lining, the rainbow after the rainstorm. Positivity is not pretending pain isn't real or that suffering isn't hard. Positivity is accepting the full spectrum of our emotions and the cycles of life—that this too shall pass. Which, by the way, was always one of my least favorite sayings! I felt like it sometimes trivialized the hard moments. But there is such wisdom in it and it's a mantra that has certainly helped many hang on during the hard parts.

Chronic illness, stress, and, yes, this chronic pandemic, has some of us asking, "When will it pass, and how will it pass?" When we can't control what is happening around us and to us, when we can't control our body, particularly, we have to work extra hard to control what we can—our mindset, our emotions, and our reactions. Our attitude. Our self.

Lessons Learned

- You are the expert on yourself—be your own advocate.
- Save yourself.
- We all have limitations.
- You have to find ways to still be you.
- Attitude is everything.
- Small wins are still wins.
- Go slow but keep going.
- Not everyone will understand.
- Listen to the whispers.
- Embrace the new normal.

Make it a Mantra (Repeat after me, Doll.)

- One step at a time.
- I am calm and in control.
- I support myself with love and compassion.
- I am thankful for my body and everything it can do.
- I am healthy, happy, and full of energy.
- I release all dis-ease from my body and welcome vibrant health, love, peace, and joy.
- My sleep is relaxing and refreshing.
- I am surrounded by healing energy.
- I embrace the wisdom of my body and listen to the whispers.
- I am grateful to be alive.
- I appreciate and love my body.
- I grow healthier, stronger, and wiser with age.
- I radiate well-being.
- Every cell in my body is working in harmony.
- I shine from the inside out.
- Taking care of myself is my top priority.
- My body knows what it needs.
- My mind is free from worry and my body is free from tension.
- I honor how I feel.
- Tomorrow is a new day.

Powerful Questions:

- Have you been impacted by a health crisis?
- What can a health crisis teach us about compassion?
- Are you taking your body for granted?

- How do you feel when you wake up?
- What is your stress level like?
- Do you have a self-care routine?
- How can you support those struggling with their health?
- When you look back on your health history and your own journey towards well-being, what stands out to you?
- What changes can you make that would have the biggest impact on your health and well-being?
- What does your body know that you are resisting?

Journal

_____

_____

_____

_____

_____

_____

_____

_____

_____

_____

_____

_____

_____

_____

_____

_____

_____

_____

_____

_____

_____

_____

Journal

Journal

_____

_____

_____

_____

_____

_____

_____

_____

_____

_____

_____

_____

_____

_____

_____

_____

_____

_____

_____

_____

_____

_____

Chapter 2

SELF
IT ALL COMES DOWN TO YOU

TIME IS ONE THING MOST OF US HAD A LOT MORE OF AT THE start of the pandemic. How comfortable were you with being slowed down? As I have mentioned in the first chapter, being sick forced me to slow down, and I didn't always like it. While I have always needed my space and downtime to recharge, I am energized and lifted-up by being around others. Most of us in our modern world are used to going and doing and running around to a much greater extent than in almost every century before us. Our pace of life moves quickly.

Delivery, on-demand, instant access, and constant connectivity have made life so much easier, but they have also increased this idea of speed. When we want something, we expect it immediately. We don't always have time to plan or wait, and the more we don't have to wait, the more we can't bear it. My husband likes to joke that there is an Amazon drone that hovers above our house. Now, if I can't get something delivered the next day, I'm annoyed.

I'm so grateful for online shopping and grocery delivery. Grocery delivery was a blessing during the pandemic. While sometimes pricey, it helped me to conserve energy and took something off my husband's plate when I wasn't well. How I wished we had it years ago. Man, it would have been so helpful when my son was little to have had my meds delivered. Just thinking about how I would drag myself and him to Walgreens exhausts me. There were days when it was the only outing I'd make, and it would take all I had to pull it off.

I also wish we had these options when my grandmothers were alive. It would have made their lives so much easier when they were housebound. My sister and I used to take my Grandma O'Brien to the grocery store regularly. It was one of the few times she'd get out each week. I was in my twenties and a new manager, dating my husband; my life very much centered around my friends. I can remember being frustrated with how long she would take at Tom Thumb. I was amazed at how she knew all the workers' names. There were times when she would go by taxi. I wondered if it was then that she got to know everyone. Or maybe she seemed like she did because she always called everybody "Dear," and loved to engage and laugh and connect. I wanted to get in and out and get back to my life. As much as I adored time with my grandmother, I wanted to be at brunch with my friends, not taking her to run errands. Everything always took so much longer than the same tasks took me. I did not appreciate that this was a part of her social interaction.

With my other grandmother, I was a mother when she came to live with my mom, so my patience was different. I was used to toddler time when walking to the corner could take twenty minutes as my son toddled at his own pace and explored. My life wasn't as rooted in what my friends and others were doing anymore. It was rooted at home.

I cannot tell you how much I regret the way I felt with my Grandma O'Brien. Don't get me wrong; I have many wonderful memories and I know I was a good granddaughter, but what I wouldn't give to spend a day running errands with her now.

The pandemic has given us all a glimpse into what it's like to be housebound. It's hard. It's isolating. It can be boring. And so many of our elderly are living this way.

In college, I studied abroad, in Barcelona, for the second semester of my Junior Year. It was one of the most amazing experiences of my life, but it didn't start that way. It started out being super stressful and a bit depressing. I felt great being able to function in a foreign country while speaking a foreign language that, as it turns out, I knew so much better than I realized. But it was exhausting. I struggled so badly with the time-change, and I sometimes had a headache after working so hard at speaking and listening to Spanish all day.

Like any new experience, I had to figure out all of the basics: how to get to class, where to buy what I needed, how to adjust to living with new people, and making new friends. I suppose it was a bit of a culture shock for me. The differences weren't a negative, but they were still adjustments I had to make. I felt stretched. And I was alone. I didn't have my support system on hand and nothing was familiar. It was awfully expensive to make international calls or to even make a regular phone call in Spain back then, so I only spoke to my parents once a week. And letters took a long time to arrive. I felt lonely in my room at night working on homework.

By the end of the first two weeks, I had started getting to know another girl who lived down the street from me. We had been walking to and from school together daily and hanging out a bit each day. As we started talking about the adjustment to Spain, I finally said out loud how I was feeling a bit depressed, even though I was happy and grateful to be studying abroad.

Novel and new experiences help us to stretch and grow.

The contrast of how I was feeling didn't make sense to me. As I was talking it out, it dawned on me that I hadn't hugged anyone since I said good-bye to my family the day that I left the United States. My adorable, high-energy friend right then and there grabbed me and gave me a big hug. She laughed and promised to hug me every day if it would help.

It was a weird epiphany of how much physical touch mattered to me—that I needed it. I was like a wilting plant. When I share this story with close friends, it doesn't come as a surprise. Everyone knows I am a touchy-feely person, but until that moment outside the **Fundació Joan Miró** art museum in Barcelona I didn't *know it,* know it.

My point is that novel and new experiences help us to stretch and grow. Doing new things or stepping outside our comfort zone can be hard. But hard times, moments of struggling—both big and small—help us to learn about ourselves. And when we go through these things alone, away from our normal structures and support, we often learn the most about ourselves.

The pandemic, while uncharted waters, has been such a challenge. Not because we were in a new environment, but because we were all stuck in place without an end in sight.

Rather than having to explore ourselves in new situations, this challenge forced us to deal with ourselves while trapped in our own environment.

The isolation that came from social distancing has been extremely hard for many. Even when in a house full of people, the general isolation and slower pace have been hard. This is in part because we are social creatures who need physical interaction, but it's also because all those other people, the activity, the have-to-go-and-dos, all that noise, all that busyness can be a great distraction from dealing with ourselves.

When we are slowed down, when we feel stuck, we naturally start to assess where we are. When we are held in place and can't avoid looking at ourselves in the mirror, staring at the same four walls, the things we like and don't like, the things we need and have lost, the things we want and we lack, all tend to be more glaring.

Some of the ways we would have dealt with feeling stuck were no longer possible in the pandemic. You couldn't just escape to a movie, run out and see a friend, or try a little retail therapy. You had to stay home and sit in it.

One of the biggest challenges with the pandemic was that we had no idea of the timeline. How long will it last? When will life return to normal? How can I make the things I want to happen, happen when I am stuck inside my house? Stuck inside my head? The "this too shall pass" mantra gets harder when it seems like things will never pass.

For our extroverts and people-oriented folks, not having that social connection and in-person interactions during shelter-in-place, including ongoing social distancing, was a big challenge. Like I felt in Spain, they too felt like a plant that's going without water and sunlight. Shriveled, sad, anemic.

Our task-oriented friends also struggled. They may have knocked it out of the park the first few weeks with uber productivity; whipping the whole house into shape, getting organized, starting a vegetable garden, and baking bread. But over time, the lack of control and ability to go charging forward and accomplish things in ways they are used to probably also felt limiting.

Some people joked that as introverts they had been training for shelter-in-place their whole lives. But even introverts struggled. Many introverts are still people-oriented. They may not need to be in the company of lots of people, or as frequently as extroverts, but they typically have a close-knit crew that is significant. And imagine being an introvert who recharges through solitary time and being "stuck" with your entire family at home all day every day. Might make you a little crabby, right, Doll?

Again, we know these things about ourselves, but like being abroad for the first time, or at home with a newborn, or convalescing after surgery, when isolated, alone, and or in stressful, more extreme scenarios, these fundamental truths about ourselves become more glaring. Sometimes our needs and reactions surprise us, and we start to realize—to get really clear—about what is most important to us. What we need most. That starts again with acceptance of who we are and what we need.

WHO ARE YOU REALLY?

So, who are you, Doll? And what do you—amazing and fabulous you—want and need? This is the ultimate question of the pandemic. Frankly, it's the ultimate question, period. What is essential to you?

If I were to ask you the question, "Who are you?" or the age-old interview question, "Tell me about yourself," you'd likely start to answer it as it relates to others. I'm a wife. I'm a mother. I'm a daughter. Or in the form of labels. I'm married. I'm divorced. I'm chronically ill. I'm dyslexic. Or what you do. I'm a high school student. I work in HR. I'm a designer. I manage a bank.

What I want to know is who ARE you? Who are you when it's all stripped away? Who are you at your core? Who are you whether you are at home or in a foreign country? Married or single? Who are you? Who are you when your kids are grown, and your grandkids are building their lives, your spouse and oldest friends are gone? Who are you in the end, in the beginning, and in the middle, when you are all alone?

If you are getting sad, or panicked, or are starting to feel like you are now standing in your living room naked, like there's a weirdly uncomfortable spotlight on you, then it's time to delve deeper. To fight past the existential dread. The existential fear of being alone. Of being who we are. Claiming who we are deep down inside can be scary. It can feel harder than it probably should to put it into words. And many of us have been conditioned to ignore it.

What I want you to be really clear about, and unafraid of, is claiming and stating what makes you, *you*. You are unique. There are many mothers, marketers, daughters. What makes you, *you*? What makes you the special mother, marketer, daughter combo that you are? What are your unique traits, strengths, and style? What are your values, dreams, and goals? What are your top priorities, and is your life in alignment with them? Does your life reflect your true self and what is essential to you?

And do you like yourself? Would you choose yourself as a friend or partner? Do you like, value, and trust yourself? Do you enjoy your own company?

Those whispers of discomfort—don't be afraid of them.

When you pause and assess, you may find things are not in alignment. I don't mean in the outside forces of the pandemic kind of way. I mean internally and how you have created and ordered your life.

When you pause and reflect, you may find that who you are now is quite different from who you once were, and who you want to be may look different still. How does it feel when you think about this? Do you feel generally good and grateful? If so, hooray! Big hugs and pats on the back. Celebrate yourself! Do a little happy dance.

If you are not feeling great about who you are, that's OK too, Doll. You still get to celebrate yourself. You still deserve a great big hug; so wrap your arms around you. Knowledge, as the saying goes, is power. Once we accept ourselves as we are, where we are, then we can shift and change and grow. Those whispers of discomfort—don't be afraid of them. Give into them. Surrender to what they are telling you to do. Those are the emotional signposts that say you are in transition. And remember what I was told? That's right, a new birth is well on its way!

HAPPY BIRTHDAY

Ask any woman and they will tell you that giving birth is scary. And it's hard work. That, of course, is why they call it labor.

Giving birth is also freaking messy. Really messy. Like, kind of gross. It's also magical and empowering. It is life. And here's the big thing, it takes whatever amount of time it takes. This is so important. Some of us labor for five mad dash intense hours and others labor for days. The process is the process, and it will go at its own pace.

This is why comparing your birth experience to someone else's may be interesting, but irrelevant. If you look at another birth and say, mine is going way too fast, something's wrong, or mine is going way too slow, I'm not doing something right, it will not change or help your birth. It will not change your timing. Like actual childbirth, we never know how long it will take. When it comes to birthing our own new lives it may take days, months, or even years. What you can count on is a shit ton of pushing hard, probably some pain, and, of course, reminding yourself repeatedly to breathe.

When we are in pain, afraid, or upset we so often hold our breath when what we most need to do is to breathe through it. Our breath is the link between our mind and our body. It helps us to relax, pause, and recenter. When you start to feel overloaded, either physically, mentally, or emotionally, it is time to pause and breathe. When you are giving birth, you can feel flooded in any of these three ways, at any given moment, or all at once. That is why breathing is so important. Even the most superhuman among us, a Navy Seal, for instance, can only hold their breath for a few minutes because breath is life. So, stop holding your breath—breathe through it and into it and allow life to transform from pain to beauty, from labor to birth.

Yet, even as beautiful as birth is, there's often a fear of birthing new life. So often, our rebirths are created because of a crisis: the death of a loved one, divorce, getting sober, job loss. Oh, I don't know, maybe even a pandemic. Many times, however, it's also the result of natural shifts we go through in life, like becoming a parent, graduating from school, or a milestone birthday—the old mid-life crisis cliché. Both these natural shifts and the big critical losses strip away one of our identities or labels. When we either outgrow them or have no choice but to give up those labels, we are forced to face the question of who we are. Who am I still? Who do I want to be? How can I adapt to where I find myself? How will I define myself in this next chapter of my life? Who am I now?

We tend to either embrace or resist these moments. When we resist what is already happening or has happened, we get stuck—stuck trying to fight, delay, or prevent the moment of transition. Fighting it means staying in the height of pain and exhaustion or staying stuck in a place that no longer fits. It also means that we are delaying what is on the other side, that new life full of possibilities.

While we have to accept that we can't control everything that happens to us, when we are fixated on the idea that things are happening to us and that those things are unfair, unwanted, or undeserved, it reinforces the feeling that there isn't anything we can do about it, and so we feel stuck. Ho-hum. Woe is me. Can you feel the weight of that? It's depressing. It's a slog. It begins to impact your mindset so that you can't see a way forward.

Take aging, for example. A transition every one of us must go through. It's a natural part of life that happens whether we like it or not, but it can feel like something that is happening to us. Like it's mean. Like it's somehow unfair, unwanted. Yes, it's outside of our control, but it is supposed to happen. It is knowable that it will occur. Yet, many of us wish for what once was, rather than acknowledging and accepting what now is.

And it's OK to miss and mourn what was. It's OK to remember it fondly—to even wish you had fully appreciated the beauty, strength, impact, importance of that time. But why miss the beauty, strength, impact, importance of this moment wishing for the past or hoping for the future?

I will never forget a conversation I had with my grandma when she was close to 90 and I was in my 40s. She was telling me how she missed being 60 and how great she looked and felt at 60! It is all relative, Doll! When my grandma told me this, it immediately made me think of a photo I had recently found from when I was about 25.

I distinctly remember that day when we picked up the photos. (Yes, this was back when same-day photo development and doubles was a thing that still amazed and delighted us.) That perfect summer weekend in Boston had been a blast with my college roommate, my brother, and his college teammates. I was wearing a beige miniskirt that I adored and felt great in. But I remember looking at this super cute photo of the three of us sitting on the couch in an apartment off Newbury Street and thinking, *Oh, my god, my thighs look fat.*

Now, there I was in my 40s not long before the perspective-shifting convo with my grandma, and I had come across this same photo but did not see one ounce of fat, not even dimpling on those 25-year-old thighs! Why had I seen myself through such a critical lens back then? Nothing about that photo or my memory of that amazingly fun weekend had changed. But I saw myself differently in my 40s. And the only thing that had changed was my perspective. My mindset.

We can be our own worst critics. We can be judging ourselves through an out of focused lens, leading us to not fully appreciate our gifts and each important phase of our lives. The good news is that we can get our mindset right if we admit how we feel and why.

Before the pandemic, many people knew they needed to make some changes in their lives. Maybe you and your partner had reached the point of accepting that your marriage was irreparable. Then came the pandemic and one of you lost your job, so you decided it's better to continue muddling through to have insurance and protect your finances. What steps can you take now that divorce is off the table?

You can create a budget, organize your things, map out a vision for your new life. You can work on your communication skills so that you can be stronger co-parents. You can start working towards forgiveness of whatever mistakes and disappointments played a part in you falling out of love. You can go to therapy. You can reprioritize another goal. You may not be separating for now, but you can plan and prepare and be ready to move forward as soon as things shift. You can control what you can, or you can be miserable and pout because you can't get divorced right now. We can make life harder or easier for ourselves depending on how we react to it.

I knew I should have switched jobs sooner. I should have divorced him years ago. If only I had ... I am so stupid. I'm a failure. I should have. I shouldn't have. Ruminating and negative self-talk are two of the ways that many of us unintentionally relegate ourselves to the sidelines. Like we somehow missed the boat and can, therefore, never get on another one.

WE ALL FALL DOWN

When our kids are learning to walk and run, what do we say to them when they fall down? "It's OK, you're alright." We don't want them to be afraid of falling. We teach them to get back up, brush it off, and keep going. Well, that is really the ultimate life lesson. We will trip. We will stumble. We will get knocked down. And we will fall flat on our faces. But we can and we must brush ourselves off and keep going. That's living. That's surviving. That's resilience. It's the lesson we've learned since we first started to be a little bit independent and wobbled away from our parents. So why are so many of us so afraid of falling?

And, certainly, we'd never say to a toddler, "You are so stupid, I can't believe you fell!" So why do we so often speak to ourselves in these harsh and horrible ways?

For the toddler who is supported in their newfound skills and freedom to move about, I'm sure in their little brains, they learn, "I remember that one time when I fell and it hurt, I was scared, shocked, embarrassed, but I got up and walked again. I did it. And then I felt good. I felt happy. I forgot all about falling earlier. I feel proud of myself. I'm smiling. I'm off and running and doing what I hoped to do." Maybe not in those words, but that is what they are learning.

This is how resilience is built. One step, one stumble, then one step again. Through mistakes. Through trial and error. We get knocked down. We get back up again. And we know that if we got up once before we can do it again. Resilience is built one imperfect, wobbly step at a time. Through gumption. Through trying again and getting better and stronger.

Ultimately, resilience hinges on self-belief and self-trust. This is why a crisis, while painful, can be so powerful. We are

tried and tested. It's helpful when we have support
to give us a hand when we
fall, or to cheer us on when
we get back up, but we have
to know and believe that
when we don't have some-
one else to figure it out

**If you don't believe in
yourself, who will?**

for us, when we don't have anyone but ourselves to lean on,
we can still do it. We can dig in deep, dust ourselves off, and
try again.

We have to draw on our strengths, our past experiences,
and the wisdom of those who have shaped us and rise to the
occasion. And we can and should be our own cheerleaders
telling ourselves, "It's alright, you're OK, you can do it." If you
don't believe in yourself, who will?

Remember when I mentioned listing everything I had
done—even the most basic things? This same idea can help
us when we are afraid. We can remind ourselves of every hard
thing we have done, every other challenge we have faced,
however imperfectly we faced them, and remind ourselves
what we did right, what we learned, and that we can meet the
next challenge from a place of greater knowledge, experience,
and confidence.

How we speak to ourselves is critical because it correlates
to how we feel about ourselves and the fullness of our own
personal expressions. Our relationship with ourselves is at
the heart of our ability to cope with crises. And, frankly, it's
at the heart of all our other relationships. You can't expect
others to understand who you are and what you need if you
can't name it, own it, and step fully into it yourself. The same

way, you can't communicate openly and honestly with others if you aren't being honest with yourself.

Lessons Learned

- Wherever you go, or don't go, there you are.
- Challenges are opportunities to learn and grow.
- Sometimes you need to push; sometimes you need to pause and breathe.
- Control what you can.
- Life will never be perfect, but the right mindset and attitude make it easier.
- You don't have to have all the answers to move forward.
- Self-limiting beliefs and old stories keep us stuck.
- Watch for the emotional signposts.
- Be your own greatest labor of love.
- If you don't believe in yourself who will?

Make it a Mantra. (Repeat after me, Doll.)

- It's OK to go it alone.
- I trust the divine timing of my life.
- I've made it through before and I'll make it through again.
- I trust myself to make the best decisions for me.
- I listen to my heart and my intuition. I trust my instincts.
- I know what I want and what I need to do.
- What I need and want matters.
- I am focused on my goals.
- I am grateful for all I have.

- My spirit leads me.
- I deserve the best in life.
- I am optimistic. I stay positive.
- I am beautiful inside and out.
- I am focused on the present.
- I accept myself.
- I can begin again.
- I am free to be myself.
- I am worthy.
- I have the power to shape my life.
- I am never alone. I am connected to all that is.

Powerful Questions

- What makes you come alive?
- What has helped you get where you are today?
- What is the biggest obstacle you have had to overcome, and what did it teach you about yourself?
- Who are you when you are most proud of yourself?
- What parts of your life need an upgrade?
- What is your daily self-talk like?
- What would you most like to accomplish in life?
- How are you holding yourself back?
- How do you want to be remembered?
- What are three goals you can set for yourself right now?

Journal

_____

_____

_____

_____

_____

_____

_____

_____

_____

_____

_____

_____

_____

_____

_____

_____

_____

_____

_____

_____

_____

_____

_____

Journal

_____

_____

_____

_____

_____

_____

_____

_____

_____

_____

_____

_____

_____

_____

_____

_____

_____

_____

_____

_____

_____

_____

Journal

_____

_____

_____

_____

_____

_____

_____

_____

_____

_____

_____

_____

_____

_____

_____

_____

_____

_____

_____

_____

_____

_____

_____

Chapter 3

RELATIONSHIPS
RELATE WELL. LIVE WELL.

THE PANDEMIC CREATED A LOT OF TOGETHERNESS. FOR some families, like mine, it was a welcome surprise to have more time together. My son is in high school, and I was secretly happy to have him around more. I'd like to keep him here for a few more years. Sure, he's still hiding out in his room most of the time, but I love hearing his laughter and just knowing that he's in the house, because I know my days are numbered and college is not far off.

That said, as much as I was enjoying having everyone around, I still had my moments when I longed to be alone. *For just like a day,* I would think to myself. *Like back in the good old days when people went to school and work, and I was home alone for seven glorious hours.*

And my goodness, the folks with multi-generations under one roof or littles cooped up and going crazy! Single parents, my heart went out to you. It wasn't easy for many of us. We all had our moments when we just couldn't do it anymore with these people.

Beyond the challenges of our immediate family under one roof nonstop, the pandemic created strains on our other relationships. We are living in a highly polarized time and the pandemic became one more area of polarization. At a time when we needed to connect virtually with our family and friends, our social media posts seemed to showcase our differences and highlight some challenges that were already there.

Rather than enjoying the highlights and family photos of one another's lives, we became overly attuned to beliefs that always existed. And when expressed in posts or memes, they are recorded and reviewed in our minds in a much more intense way. Rather than connecting us and bringing us together, social media seems to be pulling us apart.

The advice used to be don't talk politics around the dinner table. Now we're being pulled into one-sided conversations all the time online. Imagine what these repeated messages, that cause us surprise, shock, or disgust, do to our brains. What does the validation of our beliefs or witty quips do to artificially inflate our sense of self, to reinforce our position? What does it do to our dopamine levels and our stress hormones?

Now add to that a problem with no immediate solution, and we have had a not so winning combination. The virus seems to have attacked not only our immune systems but also our support systems, exposing fault lines and feeding so much anxiety and strife.

I had been sick too many times with hard-to-treat illnesses not to take COVID seriously. It took three surgeries and tons of antibiotics and steroids to rid my body of MRSA. And for the first two and a half of the five months that I had whooping cough, the ER, three specialists, and my regular doctor struggled to identify it. So, I didn't care if many of the COVID cases were mild. I didn't want it at all, in any form.

I spent five days isolated from everyone while being treated with radioactive iodine for my thyroid cancer. Talk about depressing. To feel sick, anxious, and alone is beyond miserable. I don't want to live like that again. My mother was in the hospital for a week after the numbers in Dallas had surged enough to force stronger mask and social distancing mandates. We could not be at the hospital with her, and she needed an advocate. I didn't want to go through that with a disease that doesn't have a proven protocol. (Um, Guess what? I still got it. Because—that's right, Doll—we are not in control!)

So, yes, my family and I went hard-core with the COVID precautions. We eased up after three months near the end of June to see family and recharge at the ocean. We did it as carefully as possible, but we took more chances than we had before. And we needed it. That balance between taking care of yourself physically and taking care of yourself emotionally can be hard to navigate, but there comes a point when we all have to re-evaluate and choose.

I chose to take a risk to see the most important people in my life—my family. When we started seeing friends, even outside and socially distanced, it was only with people I knew were like-minded. But even that got challenging as weeks went by.

From the outset, there were people in my community that didn't take it as seriously. I'm sure it was the same situation in your community. We were headed into spring break when things escalated internationally and domestically. The kids left for spring break on a Friday and never returned to school.

But many families still travelled. Others let their kids hang out with friends daily.

Most people were understanding and respectful of our choices, especially knowing my health history. But I'm sure some people thought I was going overboard. And as we moved into the fall and did more, we still had a few friends who were keeping to the highest levels of social distancing, and they probably questioned our choices and second-guessed seeing us.

For some friendships, the pandemic meant forced separation because they agreed it was the right thing for their families and society at large. For others, it meant forced separation because they disagreed with which precautions were necessary. And for those already in complicated or strained relationships, the pandemic placed an even greater strain. For others, time alone and apart from the usual suspects led to reassessing who they had been prioritizing and what relationships they were and weren't missing.

Crisis can do this. Crisis finds the cracks and widens them. This is not to say that crisis can't bring us together. It can and it does. Think 9/11. Or a family who loses their house in a fire and the whole community comes out to clothe and shelter them. There are times when we rally together, but when crises become chronic, they have a greater chance of eroding a rocky foundation. And chronic crises—long-lasting, persistent, and pervasive—can chip away at us when our coping clashes.

For example, during the longest stretches of my worst health periods, my husband held on to the idea of being stoic. He kept his head down and trudged forward in the face of resistance. He felt there were no options but to keep on keeping on and pulled inward to have the energy to keep going.

The year I had four surgeries pretty much pushed us over the edge. It had been seven, almost eight, years since my cancer diagnosis and four or five years into living with my autoimmune illnesses. The daily struggles over months and years were taking their toll. We struggled to communicate, to find the time and the energy to try. We were so far out of sync, both of us in our own worlds coping as best as we could. It was not good, and it was so hard to find ways to reconnect and recharge when everything felt like a struggle and life felt so limiting.

I was isolated much of the time during that particular year. Of course, I had a small circle of family and close friends with whom I spent my time, but I couldn't and didn't do much. I didn't feel well physically, I didn't feel good about how I looked either. I had been back at work part-time for a while, but it had been too hard with all the surgeries—two of which had months-long recoveries. Once again, I stopped working, which took a toll on my self-esteem. I felt like a quitter. I felt incapable of what others managed. I wasn't living a full life on my own terms and that was hard.

What I learned the hard way was that when our coping is strained, or gets pushed to the limit, it ends up straining our relationships. So often, we pull away instead of coming together. I wish I had known then, what I know now about personality styles. It would have helped me to have another lens through which to view how my husband and I both handled stress and communicated. Communication style clashes during the good times are not the end of the world. They may be annoying and cause little tiffs, sometimes they are even cute, but when differing communication styles cause you to slip deeper into conflict and stress, it can widen the gap when you desperately need to be bridging it.

COMING TOGETHER

We all have our innate personality styles, and they come with a set of strengths. These are our unique factory settings if you will. Understanding our styles can help us to better understand our relationships. My go-to resource for understanding personality styles is the DISC model of human behavior. There are lots of great personality assessments that each offer a distinct framework. I like them all, but in my experience, DISC is easier for people to get their heads around and that makes it easier to use in improving understanding and communication.

DISC was developed in the 1920s by Harvard psychologist, Dr. William Marston. He and other psychologists noted that human behavior is observable and measurable. DISC has been further developed over the years and there are many versions you will see because it is not owned by any one person. The descriptors may vary slightly, but all DISC resources cite the same four personality types: dominant (High D), inspiring (High I) supportive (High S), and cautious (High C), or what Marston

When we are trying to bridge the gap, connect better, and deescalate conflict in our relationships, DISC can help us by providing a common language.

originally referred to as dominance, inducement, submission, and compliance. In truth, we all have some of each type in our make-up. We are each a unique blend of these four types. Most people have a dominant trait and a secondary trait.

Many people have two secondary traits. But as an introduction to the model, let's focus on the four primary types.

When we are trying to bridge the gap, connect better, and deescalate conflict in our relationships, DISC can help us by providing a common language. It is a non-judgmental tool that allows us to analyze our filters and reframe our interactions. DISC can assist us by taking the emotion and judgement out of it, so we can be more objective about ourselves and others.

DISC Personality Styles		
High D	The Dominant Personality	Independent, plays to win, driving, doers
High I	The Inspiring Personality	Exciting, expressive, fun-loving, "people" people
High S	The Supportive Personality	Steady, sweet, sentimental, team players
High C	The Cautious Personality	Conscientious, composed, logical, rule followers

The High D Dominant Personality

The dominant personality is outgoing and fast-paced. They are task-oriented, determined, driven doers who make things happen. They get shit done and are competitive. They like and need challenges and they play to win. Dominant personalities need to be in control, which means they need choices.

Of their many strengths, they are independent, self-confident, industrious, and are often natural leaders. They are direct communicators and can be firm when they need to be.

Under stress, they can be impatient and may seem inconsiderate, although that likely is not their intent. High Ds can be opinionated and come on strong. To others, their dominant personality can seem aggressive.

A dominant personality gets bored when things slow down, so you can imagine how hard the start of the pandemic was for them. Listening is not typically their strong suit, especially when they are stressed out. In relationships, they have to be aware of their tendency to want things their way and guard against becoming too controlling. They may start micromanaging others to feel more in control and shouldn't be so focused on completing tasks or accomplishing their goals that they forget about the needs and feelings of those around them. And they need to learn how to compromise and be flexible and give other people time to process information and ideas at their own pace.

High Ds fear appearing weak and worry they will be taken advantage of. They are not afraid of confrontation but need to be careful not to be too adamant and remember that being combative is not the same as handling conflict.

If you've ever argued with a dominant personality, you'll know they are focused on winning the argument. They stress logic and don't want to give emotions the same weight. This is highly problematic if they are in a relationship with an inspiring (High I) or supportive (High S) personality who values feelings, expression, and consensus. High Ds may need help seeing the bigger picture and should mitigate their tendencies by focusing on putting the relationship first. They need to let love win.

High Ds are so driven, they should learn to give themselves permission to rest and relax and just have fun. Dominant personalities need physical activity to recover from stress, so walk, run, ride, garden, build—whatever you do, move and be active!

The High I Inspiring Personality

Like the dominant personality, the inspiring personality is also outgoing and fast-paced. They are high energy and like a lot of activity, but they can be less focused. They are people-oriented and highly emotional and expressive. Their emotional intelligence is typically quite good because they are so attuned to feelings and others.

Imaginative and intuitive, inspiring personalities feel their way through their decisions and often need to talk through their decision-making process. So, get comfortable, because as their audience you will likely be there awhile. Keep in mind that they are processing verbally more than they are looking for your advice.

But don't be fooled, they need validation. High Is are wired to need recognition and approval. In relationships, you can expect them to be open and direct when you solicit their opinion. They are generally friendly folks who love being in the mix and the center of attention. They need to be well-liked and may put the relationship above good boundaries, rules, and healthy choices. They are also adept at influencing others. They have many best friends and a great sense of humor.

You can imagine how inspiring personalities (party people) struggled with the isolation and lack of social activity during the pandemic. They may have gotten needy and annoying, prone to pouting and boredom because they need fun, excitement, and spontaneity. High Is recharge through connection; they need to find positive uplifting ways to channel their energy and sort through their emotions—blogging, podcasts, journaling, talking, and sharing. Creative hobbies can be a good antidote and a good fit for their many interests.

Under stress, despite their people and relationship orientation, they can become the aggressor and attack others verbally. High Is think fast and they make many connections and can weaponize this against you. They may be too outspoken and overly passionate about their causes, concerns, and desires. Generally, though, after they have vented their irritation, they move on. Not feeling heard or validated, however, can shut them down in a relationship.

To others, they can seem illogical, overly emotional, and just exhausting to lower-key personalities. Some inspiring personalities tend to exaggerate, which can erode trust or result in being tuned-out by others. They need to remember that talk isn't the same as action and may need to keep their excitement and optimism in check so that they don't become too impulsive.

To recharge, they need to reconnect with their people. They are energized by others and by having fun.

The High S Supportive Personality

Thank goodness for our sweet, steady, supportive high Ss! Supportive personalities are people-oriented like the high Is, but they are more introverted. They go at a slower pace and tend to be more reserved, possibly even shy, but relationships and authentic connections are especially important to them. They likely do better in smaller groups or one-on-one.

High S personalities are loyal and value teamwork and harmony. They seek stability, security, and assurance. The uncertainty and stress of this year no doubt took a toll on them. Systematic thinkers, many supportive personalities are planners, so the inability to plan during the pandemic was also likely hard. Others struggled with not being able to help others as they would have wished.

Our supportive friends and loved ones make great listeners and are sensitive to the needs of others. Sometimes too much so. They can come across as being too submissive and hesitate to speak up for themselves or ask for what they need. Because they are willing to help others and go the extra mile, they can be disappointed when others don't do the same.

High Ss are gifted with seeing all sides of a situation, but they need to ensure that they aren't enabling others. At the end of the day, they just want everyone to get along. Their fear of conflict can create a tendency for them to shut down and avoid things. In conflict or stressful situations, they need to guard against selective listening and changing the subject when uncomfortable.

When they are confronted with change, they can become overwhelmed causing them to double down and become inflexible. This response can throw others for a loop when they are so used to the supportive personalities in their life being the peacemakers. Sometimes others mistake their silence for consent. High Ss need to watch for resentment building up when they feel taken advantage of and beware of their people-pleasing tendencies. Slow to anger, they can also be slow to forgive and forget.

High Ss need to balance their sentimentality and desire for security with learning to embrace change and take some risk in life. And they need to learn to speak up and say no. Their loved ones need to understand how much supportive personalities worry about letting them down—so give your steady, supportive sweetheart the time and space to make decisions and set their priorities and boundaries. And make sure these supportive folks know how much you love and appreciate them!

High Ss need quiet, relaxing time alone to reset. So, find your coziest spot and get some extra sleep!

The High C Cautious Personality

Finally, we have conscientious, calm, cautious High C personalities. They share the introverted, systematic thoughtful nature and slower pace of the supportive types (High Ss). They also share the task-orientation of our dominant high Ds.

The cautious personality is typically the most reserved of the four personalities. They also aren't as comfortable with displays of emotion. It doesn't mean that they don't have feelings or emotions, but they keep them in check. Because of this they can seem cold to others.

High Cs need life to make sense, so the pandemic and inconsistent regulations and response, as well as the debates around correct science, may have made them crazy. Some of them may have felt disconnected from the struggles of others in the pandemic because shelter in place and solitary time felt good. They may have even created their own strict protocols, and worried about handling everything correctly. Doing things the right way really matters to them. They do not like to make mistakes.

Cautious personalities pride themselves on maintaining poise and composure. They are conformists by nature, and they want others to be consistent, dependable, and honest, too. "Compliance" was the original name for the high C personality. These folks expect everyone to play by the rules, which can make them seem uptight even if they are right.

The high C's even temper, and their ability to think through problems and details logically, brings stability to their interactions. High Cs need to be careful not to overuse restraint at the risk of becoming too emotionally distant and rigid. Let your guard down and let others in.

When they are deeply passionate about a project or topic they tend to go deep. They can be super detailed and talk at length about what interests them.

Cautious people process slowly but carefully. They value quality and accuracy and tend to process through data and analysis. If you know a high C personality, then you know that they tend to ask a lot of questions. Don't be put off by this! It doesn't mean that they doubt you. It means that they are thinking and assessing. It means that they are engaged.

High Cs can take a long time to deliberate and prepare because they value excellence and have extremely high standards for themselves and others. While their conscientiousness is to be admired, it can lead to perfectionism and burnout and "analysis paralysis" because they are so afraid of making a mistake.

To question a high Cs integrity is to deeply wound and offend them. In conflict, they can withdraw and stonewall.

Their tendency to self-isolate can leave them feeling misunderstood as others may think they are uncaring. Oftentimes people perceive them to be acting like a martyr.

Arguing with a high C can feel like you are on trial. Highly exacting, they may pick apart your word choice and focus on specifics rather than general meaning and the spirit of what you are trying to convey. High Cs need to be aware of judging others and being condescending. When interacting with others, keep the big picture in mind. Value the relationship more than being right to get along better with others.

Like the high S, they too can be overly sensitive. Again, just because they appear more logical than emotional, doesn't mean their feelings can't get hurt. Cautious personalities need to know they are valued and respected.

Our cautious family and friends need to recharge with quiet cognitive activity.

BREAKING APART

Being honest about our flaws can be hard. So can being honest about the roles we play in our relationships, especially when our natural tendencies start to get the better of us. It's so much easier to focus on the other person's flaws. But we can't change other people. We can only change ourselves. That means adapting our own styles to meet the needs of others.

Recognizing the other person's needs and fears based on the way they are wired can help us to be more compassionate and empathetic. It can also help us to articulate our needs and communicate more clearly when we focus on the other person's style preferences.

Despite working at understanding one another, or possibly even because we finally really understand each other's styles and needs, sometimes we realize it just doesn't work. We can respect and understand one another but it's not what we most need and desire in a friend or partner.

One of the hardest things is realizing that despite our best efforts, sometimes our relationships have run their course. Breaking up with friends can be just as hard as breaking up with a lover, partner, or spouse. Arguably harder, as there seems to be even less of a playbook. Sometimes, despite trying to work on our communication and other aspects of

We can't change other people. We can only change ourselves.

our relationships, we realize we are no longer compatible or growing together and can no longer meet each other's needs.

Letting go can be painful, but who you surround yourself with truly has an enormous impact on your mindset, goals, and well-being. It can be difficult to break old patterns with the same people in the same environment. The people are usually the pattern manifested, so sometimes we need to let go and leave people in the past in order to move forward.

It especially hurts when you are the one left behind. It can be maddening and heartbreaking and may even come as a complete shock at first. But usually, the signs are there. It just takes some time and space and a healthy shift in perspective to see it.

This is a huge part of developing our emotional intelligence. Understanding ourselves and others, having

Pushing people away and putting up walls isn't the same as creating new or healthy boundaries.

compassion and empathy for the other person's perspective, and seeing the role we too have played in the relationship. Like they say, it takes two to tango. We need to be able to own and understand our part. Accept what is and was and try to move on with grace.

This does not mean we walk away from everyone that has a harder flaw for us to cope with or lets us down. Pushing people away and putting up walls isn't the same as creating new or healthy boundaries.

What we should be careful of is letting things deteriorate so far that our outlook turns to contempt. When we break up, things do just that—break. They sever, shatter, fall apart, go to pieces. It can be messy and destructive. Sometimes, we'd never let go if there were still pieces to hold on to. But we want and should avoid total destruction. When it all falls apart, we need to acknowledge and process that, but we don't stay in the rubble. We crawl out, clean up, and rebuild.

Divorce is the epitome of a relationship fracturing. In real life and on the screen, we have seen the destruction so often correlated with divorce. Growing up in the 70s, people talked about "broken homes." It was like when people whispered "cancer." It was something so horrible you would never dare to speak it into existence in your own life. Now we have a more nuanced view of divorce. We recognize that, like a phoenix, many people are reborn from the ashes of divorce. And that families can still be a family even if the parents are no longer a couple.

When my parents divorced, I was in my early 20s and it broke my heart. Even as an adult child, I felt that my foundation was being destroyed. There were hurt feelings, hard moments, and it took a long time to move past those feelings. But my parents never spoke poorly of one another and never sought to undermine our relationships with the other. It was hard but we muddled through. When new partners came on the scene, that was a massive adjustment. But we all tried to be respectful, kind, and cordial.

This is not to say there weren't negative feelings, uncomfortable moments, or clashing perspectives. There were, but we each decided to try and embrace the change and get along. Over time, this turned into spending holidays together and shared support. It seems strange to some people, but it was just easier to get along. It was easier to embrace change and see where it took us.

I always imagined my kids going to my parents' house (my childhood home) for weekends, overnights, and holidays, as we did at my grandparents' house where my dad grew up. Because my parents sold the home after the divorce, it didn't turn out as I had imagined, but my son still had many sleepovers at his grandparents' houses and has many wonderful memories of those special times. And the bonus? My son had more people to love him.

Of all the unimaginable twists and turns of fate, my mom's mother, Gigi, ended up becoming very dear friends with my dad's second wife, Paula. If you had ever told me this was possible when my parents split up, I would have told you that you were KA-ra-zee, Doll. But during a time of major stress, when my mom was in the hospital getting a pacemaker put in during emergency surgery, my stepmother stepped up. I needed someone to look after my son and grandma as I rushed to the hospital to be with my mother, and she graciously chose to help.

Gigi and my stepmom had been together and visited at other family events. They bonded over both being from Massachusetts and my stepmother missed her own mother who had recently passed. Their relationship had always been pleasant, friendly. This time though they struck up a friendship as my stepmom offered to assist my grandma while my mom recovered. It was a huge help to my sister and me as we took care of my mother, our kids, and our jobs. (Shout out to my sandwich generation peeps for taking care of children and parents simultaneously!)

Gigi and Paula got their nails done and went out to lunch and bonded and continued to do so after my mom was better. They became true friends. It was a surprise to everyone, but what a nice one! My mom could have been haughty about it or threatened by it, but she chose to embrace it and be grateful for it. My dad or any one of us could have resisted what was happening between them, but instead we allowed their relationship to grow and transform. In doing so, it strengthened all our relationships.

It is exhausting to hold on to all the baggage from the past. Have you ever had to carry a pile of your own luggage up five flights of stairs? I have always been guilty of overpacking. When I worked for a student travel company, we'd go on tour to Europe every summer. There were no elevators in the modest European hotels we stayed at. I would schlepp all that stuff up and down all those flights and be so annoyed with myself for always thinking I couldn't live without it all.

Why do we think we can't live without bringing all that with us everywhere we go? Even overseas, into new lands and new experiences. Carrying all that baggage. Take only what you need in your next chapter, Doll. Let it go and lighten your load! You will thank me. Your friends and family will thank me.

Leave the past in the past. Pack the lessons, save a photo of the fun times, and move on!

Lessons Learned

- We each have our innate strengths and styles.
- In a relationship, you both have a hand in it.
- Empathy, compassion, and understanding require effort.
- Communication can make or break us.
- Change the patterns that no longer serve you.
- Your closest friends and family really do define you.
- You can't change other people. You can only change yourself.
- It's OK to outgrow people—try to do it with grace.
- Leave the past in the past.
- Allow relationships the time and space to evolve and move forward with forgiveness.

Make it a Mantra. (Repeat after me, Doll.)

- My heart is open. I receive love fully.
- I don't hold onto anger.
- I use my strengths wisely.
- I give love freely and without expectation.
- I am a good friend.

- I attract positive, happy people who bring out the best in me.
- My relationships serve the highest good for each of us.
- I release past hurts and resentments.
- I set myself free by forgiving myself and others.
- I am accepted, supported, cherished, and loved for who I really am.
- I release all judgment—my friends and family are free to be themselves.
- I have healthy boundaries and feel safe and secure in my relationships.
- I love and respect people with different points of view.
- I resolve conflict calmly and respectfully.
- I am allowed to take a break from people and reset.
- I communicate freely and openly with my family and friends.
- My family and I listen to and really hear one another.
- My partner and I respond to each other with compassion and support.
- I expect and receive great relationships.
- Those not meant for me will be removed from my life—I release them peacefully.

Powerful Questions

- Who is in your corner? (Who are the key people in your life and what do they provide for you? What are their greatest gifts and strengths?)
- How do you show up for the people in your life?
- In what ways might you be taking your partner, parent, friends, or family for granted?

- Are problems from the past still an issue in your relationship? (Is that because the patterns of behavior remain the same or because one of you can't let it go?)
- What are the deal breakers in your relationships?
- Are you able to empathize with others and see things from their perspective?
- Are there people in your life that are draining your energy?
- Do your relationships reflect who you were or who you are and want to be?
- How are your blind spots and coping patterns impacting your relationships?
- What do you want more of in your relationships?

To learn more about DISC or to take an assessment, please visit www.paperdollcommunication.com.

Journal

Journal

_____

_____

_____

_____

_____

_____

_____

_____

_____

_____

_____

_____

_____

_____

_____

_____

_____

_____

_____

_____

Journal

Chapter 4

PARENTING—
WE'RE RAISING ADULTS

THE IMPACT OF THE PARENT-CHILD RELATIONSHIP IS SO PRO-
found. It shapes our identity and self-perception and is
the foundation for all our other relationships. I hope that this
chapter will speak to you as a way of exploring your inner
child, patterns in your relationship with your parents (or
those that raised you), and where you might still need to cut
the cord. After all, childhood is the one thing we all have in
common, so even if you haven't or will never raise a child, at
the very least, you know what it's like to be a child.

And as parents, aunts, uncles, grandparents, or teachers,
we are modeling how we handle conflict, communicate, care
for others, create community, nurture, and build relationships. We are modeling our values to our children. What do
we want them to learn from us and what do we want them
to know?

How we get along with other adults greatly impacts the
children in our lives. Peace, as they say, begins at home, so to

help heal our community at large, we must do our part right where we are—within ourselves and within our home, and most certainly with the next generation.

I saw a meme once on how to be a parent now versus in the 80s. It had two columns. In the "parenting today" column there was a monster list of making sure every aspect of your child's emotional, social, mental, physical, and spiritual well-being is taken care of, including ensuring non-GMO, pesticide free organic food is on the table, etc., etc. The list for parenting in the 80s? Feed them sometimes.

Nowadays, when parents let their kids play without supervision, ride their bikes to the park, or take the subway alone, we have a name for it, "free-range" parenting. That's what my parents called, "get out of the house, you're being too loud" or "be home by dinner." What was once just called parenting has an almost marketing-like slogan now, because it's now considered a very particular brand of parenting.

There's so much pressure these days for both parents and their kids. That's the whole point of the meme I saw, right? And that pressure creates anxiety. Are we doing enough? Are we doing it right? Maybe we should be doing more? *I better sign them up for sleep-away camp, they need to volunteer, we're behind on SAT prep.* More, more, more. What else, what else, what else? That is our anxiety, propelling us forward in a frenzy. The impact of the pandemic has added fears about their mental health, learning, socialization, and too much screen time. Actually, we already had all those fears, they are just that much worse now!

We are just trying to raise happy, well-functioning, successful adults. Right? We want our kids to have healthy relationships. We want them to go to a good school so they can get a good job and make plenty of money, so they can support themselves and their future families and not want for anything. Right, Doll? Isn't that what we all want as parents? We want to set them up for success and to help them find their way in the world.

Feedback from colleges and employers suggests we may not be hitting the mark. I'll elaborate more on that in the next chapter, but for now, concerns over communication and soft skills are a common refrain. College professors and deans are sounding alarms over students' inability to navigate life without parental interference. Parental interference, even more shockingly, is showing up in the workplace. My friend told me about the time when she was managing her company's booth at a career fair and a mother was there with her daughter! It's the extreme, but parents who are calling college professors to debate grades rather than having their adult child self-advocate are on a slippery slope.

Many parents are so future-focused—so focused on accomplishment—that they're trying too hard to pave the path to success for their kids. The hovering of helicopter parenting has given rise to snowplow parents. What in heaven's name could be next? Shadow parents? Invisible cloak parenting?

LEARNED HELPLESSNESS

When you have a child with special needs[5], or one who has some challenges and isn't hitting their expected milestones, you learn about something called "learned helplessness."

When your child can't tie their shoes, or button their coat, or write their name, or speak clearly or confidently enough to communicate with other kids on the playground, you tie their shoes for them, you button their coat, you show them again how to write their name, and you stop your conversation with the other moms to walk across the playground and help your child navigate their budding friendships. And sometimes you continue doing this well past the point of needing to, so that your child automatically expects you to tie his shoes. He no longer tries and gets frustrated and gives up buttoning his coat. He just stands there and waits for his coat to be buttoned. That is learned helplessness.

If you solve every problem for your teen, your teen will not spring into action when a problem arises. She will not quickly begin brainstorming solutions. She will wait and wonder what you are going to do to fix it. She may marvel at your cleverness, your ability to make things happen. She may even be over the moon with relief and gratitude. She may be super appreciative and respectful, but she will not be capable until she has had to stop and think about what would Mom do? And how can she do that?

I remember when picking up my son from school one random day, he got into the car and said, "I can't wait to change!" with a funny but uncomfortable smirk. He pulled up his uniform shirt and sweatshirt to show me his half-zipped, way too small shorts. *What in the world?* I thought.

He had early morning basketball practice and had forgotten his school uniform shorts to change into. When he realized it, three of his friends went flying out of the locker room to the lost and found bin and came up with the micro shorts. We had a good laugh and I automatically started to say, "Why didn't you call me?" But thankfully I caught myself. He didn't call because they found a solution. It wasn't perfect, but they got the job done and he made it through the day. And, more importantly, he never again forgot his shorts.

That's not to say he's never forgotten anything else, but it's rare when he does. We are raising adults, but we're also raising humans. The goal is to anticipate problems, minimize mistakes, and know how to resolve problems or errors when they arise. Not to expect perfection.

We want our kids to be confident, and true confidence comes from knowing that we are capable. When we step in and do too much for our kids, what message are we sending them? If they think we don't believe they are capable, they start to assume that they aren't, and it can create anxiety, depression, apathy, and lowered expectations of themselves. And I'm afraid that as a culture, we are tipping over into the territory of learned helplessness with our kids.

There is already so much pressure with social media and the sheer amount required of our kids in any given week between homework, extracurriculars, and jobs, shouldn't home be their refuge? Even before the pandemic, anxiety, and depression had alarmingly been on the rise for teens[6]. The National Institutes of Health report that nearly one in three adolescents (13-18 years old)[7] will experience an anxiety disorder. The American Academy of Pediatrics theorizes three factors are impacting this upsetting trend: high expectations and pressure to succeed, a world that feels scary and threatening, and social media.

It is a hard thing to walk the line of when to push, when to pull, and when to leave your child alone. I struggle because my son doesn't seem as motivated as I was as a student, but he's doing fine. He's managing his learning differences with very few accommodations and without added support from his dad or me. He's doing that along with sports, hobbies, volunteering, learning to drive, and maintaining a good social life. So, what am I worried about? That he's possibly missing out on some edge of opportunity that slightly better grades may give him?

And was I *really* that much more studious, organized, and driven? I'm not sure if I'm not sometimes idealizing myself as a student. But the bigger question is, what would it take to get him to be more driven? Monitoring, cajoling, pushing? What might that do to our communication and relationship? What message would that send if he is doing his best?

When we were debating sending him back to school in person or continuing with online classes during the pandemic, we sought feedback from one of his teachers who confirmed that Patrick was doing fine. He told us that Patrick had the maturity and time-management skills to be virtual. So far, while possibly not as driven as I was, he is self-motivated in that he is self-managed. I don't check his portal. He knows that's his job. A problem with a grade or assignment? He calls, emails, or talks to his teacher.

I remember the first time he had to do this in about fifth grade. Thankfully, he was at a school that emphasized self-advocacy. It was a measurement we discussed at all parent-teacher conferences, so this helped us to help him get started at an early age. He was so nervous to make that first phone call and, in the age of texting and Facetime, unlike me at his age, his

It's so tempting to *do* when we need to be modeling, coaching, showing, training, teaching, supporting.

experience speaking on the phone was minimal. We wrote out what he should say and practiced, and then my husband sat with him as he made the call just in case he needed to step in for support or clarification. My son, despite his nerves, did it and felt proud of himself after.

It's so tempting to *do* when we need to be modeling, coaching, showing, training, teaching, supporting. Having our kids do it themselves with the proper safety net creates capability and teaches problem-solving. I'm not calling for parents to be hands-off but to be self-aware and intentional, and to let our kids fail and find their own way so that they build real resilience and true confidence in themselves and their intrinsic motivation.

THE GUILT HAS TO GO

I was blamed initially for my son's delays in preschool. It was suggested, by numerous people, that I was doing too much for him because I felt guilty for being sick, and he was reacting to the anxiety of having a sick mother, that I was babying him. In other words, I hadn't been doing it right. I can't tell you how horrible that felt. I already had a great deal of guilt and was grappling with a sense of loss.

I know some of you have been told the same thing or thought the same thing. If I had only been a better mom or a more aware dad, my kiddo would never have made a mistake, struggled, or failed. Whether it's sneaking out, stealing, drugs, sex, mental health struggles. Whatever it is, it's hard not to blame ourselves.

It was an internal battle for me, being so sure something was wrong and feeling bad about all I hadn't been able to do.

He had already been diagnosed with a speech delay and I knew he likely had a learning disability. I was right. No matter how sick or perfect my health was, these were going to be his struggles. No matter how sick or healthy I was, he was going to need specialized support to catch up with his peers. Still, despite knowing this intellectually, my heart was hurt. I was full of worry for his future. I knew that eventually, he'd be OK, but what would getting there look like? His self-esteem had already taken a hit and he was only five! And I felt like I had failed as a parent, somehow, simply because he was struggling.

I carried a lot of guilt for being unable to care for him when I was ill. When the day came to get the results of his testing, I cried as the neuropsychologist reviewed the 25-page report and explained to me everything we had to deal with and figure out. I was relieved and validated that we had actual diagnoses, but it was overwhelming, and I felt sad and bad and worried. My sweet precious guy. None of us want our kids to struggle. And it's extremely hard to cope with their struggles amid our own.

This is why I am forever grateful for what the doctor said to me in that meeting. I told her how little I could do with him some days and she asked me if he was safe. Yes. Was he clothed? Yes. Was he fed? Yes. Well, guess what? She said when I was ill, that was it. That was all that was expected of me. That was enough. I cannot tell you what a relief that was. To have someone bottom-line it for me. To tell me, I know you are doing all you can and it's OK. That's enough. He's fine and going to be OK.

And now I am going to say it to you, Doll. Especially you single parents and the parents who managed virtual schooling and the house and work during a pandemic, and still felt like you didn't do enough. It's OK, Doll. You did the best you could. You are doing the best you can. And sometimes, especially in moments of crisis or challenge, that's all we can do.

It's OK if the schedule goes to shit one day. It's OK if your kid exceeds screen time by an ungodly amount. Even for weeks on end. This too will pass, and they will be OK. You do what it takes to get through sometimes. And that's OK.

This is the really hard work of being a parent. Caring for your child and yourself. Finding the time and a private space to just cry when you need to. To give them what they need and still find a way to give yourself what you need. Sometimes, you have to put yourself first. If you don't, and you break, it will be far worse for you all than the delayed or minimal fulfillment of their needs. Sometimes, Mommy is the one who needs a time out.

Mom guilt is real and not just for working moms but for stay-at-home moms as well. (There's research indicating working dads feel it too.[8]) This feeling that they aren't doing it well enough, aren't good enough, is a feeling all too many of us have experienced or are experiencing right now. The self-doubt and heartache we feel when our kids are struggling or in crisis only intensifies this. One study that came out of England years ago, stated that nearly all mothers experience guilt at some point and, over a fifth of all moms said they feel guilty all the time[9]. All the time! That's awful.

Back in the 70s when we walked home from elementary school, let ourselves in, got a snack and watched reruns of *The Brady Bunch* because my mom was playing tennis, I don't think she ever felt guilty. Most parents will likely have some regrets. Some moments where in hindsight they would have handled something differently, but there are no perfect parents because there are no perfect people. We should not as parents feel guilty for not being with our kids all the time. We should not feel guilty as parents for wanting to take a bath, or exercise, or just be alone for a little bit.

We should not feel guilty for missing a game or performance. There are times when there are scheduling conflicts and competing priorities. One of my favorite sports memories (so far) with my son was not from a game I attended. I was sick at home in bed, and I was feeling bad about it. I felt so conflicted for missing another game, while he, on the other hand, came home and ran into my room, face beaming and told me they had won the game. He was so proud and so happy and so excited to share it with me. He was glowing. I can see his face as I write this. Joy, excitement, pride. The biggest smile. I can still hear him calling my name from the hall. The moment was that special.

I still want to be at all his games and events, but I long accepted that I can't always be there. That morning helped me to release the guilt. I was still sharing in his life. Getting to tell me made it feel like he was winning twice. We both won that morning.

PICK YOUR BATTLES

Recently, basketball has been the spark for one of my other big awakenings as a parent. My son wanted to quit playing for his high school basketball team and my husband and I really didn't want him to. We had good arguments as to why and the fact that we both strongly felt the same way probably contributed to us doubling down on pushing him to stay on the team. That pressure and frustration got to him, and when one night he came into my room stressed out and upset, I wondered if we had made a mistake taking such a firm stance.

Patrick's been an easy teen (knock on wood!). I'd like to think it's my amazing parenting, and of course, my husband gets some credit, too, but truly a lot of it is his disposition. And I think what he went through as a little kid—facing his learning challenges and dealing with my health issues—strengthened our relationship. But, we'd never gone through a power struggle. Were we making a mistake engaging in one over the basketball team?

I quit sports in high school and regretted it. I didn't want him to have that same feeling. Add to that virtual schooling, we just wanted him to stay connected. We wanted him to have a reason to occasionally leave his bedroom and get exercise. But his interests are shifting, and his workload and his busy schedule were getting to him. If he didn't like playing, why were we forcing him?

My husband and I were shocked at how sad we both felt at the thought of him not playing. We like feeling connected to the school. We like being in the gym with family and friends and watching him play. We enjoy the feeling that he's part of the team. The fun of being with everyone, the cheerleaders, soaking in all the school spirit. Was this about what was best for him or what we had envisioned for him? Was this about what he wanted, liked, and enjoyed, or what we wanted?

I felt the initial pangs of what I expect to experience when our nest is empty and I realized that while we have never felt like our identity was tied to his, the idea of not going to basketball games made me feel like I would have less to enjoy and share with him during his high school experience—less time in a community that was built around him. My heart ached a bit. And, thankfully, he chose to stick with it.

Where our identities end and our children's identities begin, can get a little blurry for parents.

Where our identities end and our children's identities begin, can get a little blurry for parents. Managing our need for our kids to achieve, and to explore what that means to us, is the hard work we each need to do as parents. We must ask ourselves what true success in life looks like. Do we need it for them or for ourselves? For our own self-worth?

What my son wants out of his high school experience may be different from what I want for him. I need to be OK with that. The goal is to lead and guide our kids so they can eventually lead and guide themselves. If we never let them start reading the map and navigating, they won't have the confidence to get there themselves. We have to get out of their way and walk alongside them until they are ready to march off on their own. It's easier said than done.

This was basketball. Not the hard kind of disconnect between who we think our kid is and should be versus what they think they want and are exploring. We need to be mindful of our needs versus theirs. As a career coach, I am always encouraging people to name and develop their strengths and invest in their interests. I realize I must be prepared to do the same for my son. I know that is how people develop their best professional selves and build fulfilling lives. And, again, that's the real goal, isn't it?

What I want more than anything is for my son to know, trust, and honestly believe that I will be there for him no matter what. While I can't protect him from everything, I can always be the safe place to land. I want him to be who he truly is and that means giving him the space to decide some of that for himself and the space to explore it.

Part of our anxiety is in thinking that if we do it all right and give our kids every opportunity, they won't struggle. They won't fail. But that's not realistic. Part of our anxiety is thinking we can and must protect our kids from everything. It's not possible. Certainly, we try. We don't let toddlers run into traffic. We use seatbelts. But there is a false notion that by monitoring and hovering, we are protecting. And then that creates that feeling that you must be doing that all the time. Then that contributes to being enmeshed, and anxious, and exhausted. As parents, we need to find a way to always be there for our kids without always being there.

As parents, we need to find a way to always be there for our kids without always being there.

While I have stressed that self-care isn't selfish and that we need to say goodbye to guilt, it is important to be present for our kids. Again, I don't mean being at their disposal like a lady in waiting, 24/7, anticipating their every need. Or, orchestrating everything and double-checking that they are on track and on task. No one likes a micromanager. Nor should we be their private security detail, tracking their every move, clearing the traffic to ensure safer travel. But to be present through connecting and giving them our time and full attention.

We need to let them explore what speaks to them and take the time to learn what that is and what it means to them. We need to play the games they want to play when they are little and listen to the music, the stories, the things our teens like and capture their interest. If your teen takes the time to talk to you, you had better stop what you are doing and soak it in. Social media, constant connectivity, and not getting a break from the social pressures of teenage life is a burden for our kids. Their homes must be a haven where they can explore who they are and who they want to be.

We want them to know that we like them and want to know them as a person. That we believe in them, that they have great ideas. That their feelings are real and important and that they can overcome what life throws at them. That they are capable of handling setbacks, and, perhaps most importantly that in a crisis they can feel safe to come to us. If we don't make the space to nurture strong communication and regular interaction with them, they may shut us out when they need us the most.

Bad things will happen. Kids may make bad choices. They can't develop good judgment if they don't get a chance to exercise their judgment away from us. Our job is to help preserve their self-esteem when the going gets rough. And as we talked about, true self-esteem is gained through knowing they accomplished something themselves.

I remember when my son was excited to get his first participation trophy after his first soccer season at the Y. He was four. It wasn't many years later that he told me they were stupid. Kids know that whether it's praise or a participation trophy, that getting it just because isn't meaningful.

True self-esteem, like confidence, doesn't come from glossing over the hard stuff but from knowing you are worthy even though you may be flawed or make mistakes. That you are loved and valued for who you are at your core, not judged and deemed worthy or unworthy based on your highs and lows, your grades, and awards.

How many adults do you know who are still healing from their relationship with their parents? How many adult children are walking around still seeking validation, still looking for love and approval and acceptance for who they are? Setting our kids up for success means not placing the burden of other people's expectations (ahem, ours, Doll) on them.

Lessons Learned

- Peace begins at home.
- Get out of your own way, so your kids can find theirs.
- No one likes a micromanager.
- Guilt and anxiety have got to go.
- Self-care isn't selfish. Honoring your own needs and taking care of yourself makes you a better parent.
- Our kids don't want perfection; they want connection.
- Their dreams, interests, values, and goals may not be what you hoped for them—that's OK.
- Acceptance is the greatest gift you can give your child.
- Coach your kid(s) to be their own advocate.
- To develop good judgment, kids need opportunities to exercise it.

Make it a Mantra (Repeat after me, Doll.)

- I parent with intention and positivity.
- I have the wisdom to lead my family.

- My kids attract only healthy and loving people into their lives.
- I am the parent my children need.
- I am patient and understanding.
- I respect my child's thoughts and opinions.
- I am so thankful my child always comes to me.
- I always understand their needs and validate their feelings.
- I model self-love and self-care.
- I am a confident, calm parent.
- I grow with my children.
- I love and appreciate my child's unique talents and personality.
- I believe in my child.
- I support my children in living their truth.
- I do what is right for myself and my child(ren).
- I can handle this.
- I am doing the best that I can for my child.
- My words are loving, kind, and supportive.
- I have time to make memories and have fun with my kids.
- I don't have to raise my voice; my children respect me.
- The right thing to do and say will come to me.
- It's easy for me and my child to talk and connect.
- Our love is an unbreakable bond that sustains them when they are anxious or afraid.
- They can feel my love when we are apart.
- I trust my children.
- Our home is their haven, free from judgment.
- We are building a legacy of love.

- I embrace my child's joy and wonder and see the world anew through their eyes.
- My spouse and I are in alignment as parents.
- I co-parent with kindness, trust, cooperation, and respect.
- We agree on what is best for our child.

Powerful Questions

- What was your favorite part of your childhood?
- Is there healing from your childhood that still needs to take place? What part of yourself still needs mothering?
- Do you have the relationship you want with your parents?
- What do you most want your children to learn from you?
- What are your biggest fears as a parent?
- How could you better support or assist your child?
- How do you feel when your child struggles?
- Do you consider your child's success your success?
- What are you doing right as a parent? Where do you need to shift?
- How do your children's personalities differ from one another and from yours?
- What do you admire most about your child(ren)?

Journal

Journal

_____

_____

_____

_____

_____

_____

_____

_____

_____

_____

_____

_____

_____

_____

_____

_____

_____

_____

_____

_____

Journal

Part Two

PROFESSIONAL

Chapter 5

EDUCATION
LIVE AND LEARN

SCHOOL CERTAINLY ISN'T THE ONLY PLACE WHERE WE LEARN, but, of course, it's fundamentally where we go to learn. And, typically, school is the first place where we learn independence and how to get along and work with others, where we are exposed to new ideas and people who may be different from us. We learn how to learn, and we have a new set of adults helping to shape us. It is where we do so much of our growing up as children and adolescents in the broadest sense. This is why determining where to send our kids to school is often such a hard decision.

The challenge of how to meet their educational needs is real. In some communities, it is bananas just trying to get your kids into preschool. You are made to feel like their entire lives hinge on this one decision. The choice between public, private, homeschool, choice, magnet, or charter isn't a decision most parents had to make in the past. IB, AP, dual credit... it's a lot of pressure for parents and kids alike. The pandemic added even more into the decision matrix—in-person, hybrid, or virtual learning—weighing family members' health needs against the social and emotional well-being of their child and their ability to learn, engage, and focus online.

And just like breastfeeding or bottle, daycare, or stay-at-home parents, many who were staunchly on one side of the virtual versus in-person debate realized that their initial choice didn't fit their family or child's needs as time progressed. We all know people who started virtually, but their kids were struggling to sustain attention and maintain grades, so they ended up sending them back in person. We have friends who sent their kids in person only to be fed up with quarantine notices and rising numbers and kept them home after all.

When my son was first diagnosed with his learning differences and his speech and motor delays, his school wanted him to repeat preschool. I feared that he would go another year without getting what he needed, on top of the fact that he was anxious and often didn't want to go to school even though he loved his teachers and seeing his friends. So, I decided to pull him out of school and homeschool him for kindergarten while I figured things out.

I never dreamed that I would be a homeschooler. At the time, I had a pretty biased view about homeschooling. I learned so much about the many resources and homeschooling options available which have only grown more extensive. We had a fun year with lots of hands-on learning, but we didn't get high marks in the structure department. School was often on a delayed start and usually included a movie in the afternoon and naptime for teacher, but it was one of my favorite times as a parent. Despite the stress of my husband working out-of-state three to four days a week, trying to sell our home, and trying to figure out what Patrick needed to succeed in school, I felt very intentional as a parent.

Every story I chose, every game we played, the music we listened to, each of our activities, all took on new meaning. I was working hard to ensure that we covered a basic kindergarten curriculum and was constantly seeking to feed his brain and his body. It was a learning experience for both of us. It opened my mind to the possibility and freedom of homeschooling which helped to remove my fear about what kind of school environment would be right for him. I realized that if a traditional classroom didn't work, if he didn't get what he needed, I could yank him out and we could homeschool. It gave me confidence because the experience created new options.

THE GIFT OF TIME

Working with him as his teacher helped me to better understand his dyslexia and exactly how he was struggling. This aided me as his advocate once he returned to school. And it aided me because I just understood better. I understood just how hard it was for him and could describe his struggles with specifics.

Remember in the first chapter when I said that you never know how what you are going through will prepare you for other chapters in your life? The experience of becoming my own researcher and advocate for my health equipped me to be Patrick's advocate.

People have asked me how we figured it out so early, so many parents have struggled to get a diagnosis and many adults still struggle, unsure if they have a learning difference or attention issues. Well, it was clear to me that he was having a hard time learning his letters and writing his name, recalling a letter from one day to the next. Even holding a pencil and cutting with scissors were a struggle. Being a lefty didn't do us any favors either.

He has a January birthday, so it was right at the start of the second semester of preschool when we had his fifth birthday party, and all his little friends had signed his birthday cards. Patrick couldn't do this. Occasionally he could, but it wouldn't stick. And more than that, there was one night when he was just beside himself because he couldn't do what they were doing on *Blue's Clues*. He wanted to draw a heart for me and write his name on it. He started sobbing, saying, "I'm no good, I'm no good, I can't even make you a heart." Which, as you can imagine, Doll, broke mine.

Keeping him home gave him the gift of time his school suggested, but in a way that protected him. It allowed some of the pressure to keep up to fall away while we got him the right kind of help. Keeping him home helped Patrick regain his sense of self and I got my little boy back. I can't underscore how important keeping self-esteem intact is for people with learning differences. It's one of the reasons they are actually called disabilities.

When you are in an environment that doesn't give you what you need but tells you in various ways that you are the one with the deficiency or problem, it becomes a disability. And what happens when kids don't get what they need? They act out or fade out. One of the biggest fallacies is that if we simply send kids to school, they will get what they need. All too often they don't. And that is a crisis. That is a crisis we should all be screaming about. Our education system was not built for everyone.

The whole idea of my preschooler saying, "I'm no good" freaked me out. I feel confident no one ever said it to him. I sure hope not, but I don't think so. But hearing others being told "very good," or "good job,"

This is how easily the messages we pick up can be internalized and become the words we then tell ourselves.

or observing that they were good at what he was struggling to do, probably made him internalize it and express it as, "I am no good." At five. At FIVE! This is how easily the messages we pick up can be internalized and become the words we then tell ourselves.

This is why the mantras at the end of each chapter are so important. They are the antidote to the outdated and off-base messages we received and have repeated to ourselves for too long. Sadly, much of the real learning we do in life is unlearning.

This brings me back to my point. What happens when kids don't get what they need? When they internalize the overt and unintentional messages that they aren't as good? They act out or fade out. They find new ways to gain attention or adopt defensive behaviors to protect themselves from feeling vulnerable and from failure. Worst case scenario, they drop out completely or are kicked out.

The school-to-prison pipeline is fed through kids who are not identified and don't get the early intervention that they need. In my home state of Texas, 80% of prison inmates are functionally illiterate and 48% have dyslexia[10]. The National Council on Disability states, "Studies show that up to 85 percent of youth in juvenile detention facilities have disabilities that make them eligible for special education services, yet only 37 percent receive these services while in school."[11]

1 in 5 people have learning or attention issues[12]. If white upper-class Americans can't get the diagnosis and intervention their kid needs, do we think the Hispanic child in ESL whose parents are recent immigrants and don't speak English and have never navigated the school system, is getting what they need? I for one am not confident.

There are so many challenges in our school system rooted in the many challenges of our society—racism, poverty, immigration, disability law. Take the hard stuff out. Neurotypical kids, who come to school fed and well cared for, still have various learning challenges, and need individualized support. What I learned and know for sure is that every ability is a spectrum, but our traditional school structure isn't equipped to handle the full spectrum of learning styles, intelligence, and needs.

And while we probably agree (especially after reading the last chapter) that every kid doesn't need a trophy to feel good about themselves, every kid does need an adult who figures out what that child is interested in, likes, and enjoys, and helps to identify what they *are* good at and nurtures and supports them so that the child feels good. This way every child can feel pride in their curiosity, talents, and strengths. Every child can feel good about themselves in a healthy way.

When we sent my son back to school, we sent him to The Shelton School—a world-renowned leader in teaching intelligent kids who learn differently. I am keenly aware that this option is not available to everyone. For us, it was worth every penny. He transformed. I knew his teachers were doing more than unlocking his ability to read and write when we were at a party at my sister's house and I overheard him introduce himself to a boy around his age and he

How often are we limiting our growth and learning by other people's limited beliefs and definitions?

asked the boy, "What's your talent?" He was like a mini-Dale Carnegie. It was incredible though. Can you imagine if everyone walked around wanting to know that about one another? Encouraging that in one another?

WHAT'S YOUR TALENT?

Who am I, what do I need, how do I learn best, in what setting will I thrive? Where am I going, what am I doing next, and how do I need to be equipped? Or who is my child, what do they need, how do they learn best, in what setting will they thrive? Where will they go next and how do they need to be equipped? These are the questions we ask ourselves over and over as we are developing and going through the education system.

How we do in school, what type of learner we are, and how we are classified impact our belief in what we can do next. My mom was steered toward an Associate degree to be a secretary because, you know, that was what women did. How often are we limiting our growth and learning by other people's limited beliefs and definitions?

These labels are powerful. If you are a good student, then that means you are smart. That's what our traditional school mindset teaches us. I saw an old elementary school friend years ago. We were in our 30s. "You were in the smart classes," he said. He remembered that about me. The classifications of learning speed, while likely well-intentioned, set children up to judge one another. So often that judgment is reinforced by comments adults make. We've all heard the jokes about the short bus.

The reality, however, is that I likely also have dyslexia. I was atrocious at spelling. It made no sense to me. I only fully grasped syllables when I learned Spanish, which was much more straightforward than English. But I was excellent at grammar and diagramming sentences. My horrible spelling was mostly overlooked because my teachers knew I was smart. They weren't overly concerned by it. Why? Because I had been labeled in the positive. I was in the pilot program for the new trend in the mid to late 70s of specialized programs for "gifted and talented" students. G&T (or TAG depending on your area or the decade) saved me.

G&T gave me confidence in how I worked and learned, processed, and thought. The beautiful thing was that G&T also exposed me to different ways of learning—it was much more hands-on, exploratory, and project-based. I now recognize the power in that type of learning. I remember the projects from fourth to sixth grade better than I do almost anything else from school.

Some of my friends thought good grades came naturally to me. Not really. I studied like crazy, to the point of burning out midway through high school. Math was harder for me. I remember zoning out and playing games of matching up numbers to get married when I was in second grade because, as I already mentioned, I watched too many soap operas and because it didn't innately make sense to me. It got worse from there. I never felt super confident because my dad always did calculations so quickly—adding up the bill, calculating the tax or the tip, or whatever the case may have been, so fast. And I couldn't do it as fast as he expected me to. I always felt rushed and like my brain was short-circuiting.

In high school, I was in honors, but not top honors for math, and once I got it, I got it, but getting there in Honors Algebra I, for example, was painful. It was the first time I was ever failing a class. And my teacher was so mean. She was very uptight about exactly how we had to take notes. We were required to neatly rewrite our notes every night and they had to be underlined with colored pencils. This was part of our grade. Something with my heavy honors workload and the time it took me to solve the actual problems made no sense to me. It was an added burden and it made me resentful. Why were pretty notes important? Because that's how she liked it? That's how she learned, and she was convinced that made it the best way.

I worked hard that semester and, thanks to nightly help from my dad who helped me figure out my homework, and daily tutoring from my dear, patient friend, during our shared free period, by the end of the semester it was starting to click. And I was determined not to fail. I refused to give up. I refused to let that crotchety teacher win, and I worked my ass off.

And guess what? My teacher wasn't happy for me when I got an A on the final exam and raised my failing grade to a passing one. She was shocked and, dare I say, disappointed. I didn't pass because she taught me. I passed because I refused to not figure it out on my own with my support system. I asked for the help I needed from others who were willing to provide it.

I will never forget how hard it was for her to acknowledge my hard work and accomplishment. She chose rather to pull me out into the hall and say she was surprised that I had managed it and felt it was best that I be demoted to "regular" Algebra I for the second semester. I was all too happy to leave that woman's classroom, but guess what happened when I went back to on-level? I was bored.

Despite my teacher's reaction, my confidence in my ability was so much more rock-solid. And despite my boredom, my understanding of my ability was accurate. I knew I wasn't a math genius, but I knew I could hold my own. I knew my true skill was somewhere in between on-level and honors. I was placed back in honors for the next year, and I stuck to pre-AP, not AP, and laughably was asked to join the math honors society in my next school.

Imagine if I had not been told since elementary school that I was bright, that I was "gifted and talented," and a capable student. Imagine instead that I had encountered teacher after teacher like my Algebra I instructor who believed that I wasn't capable and had set the bar lower for me. A teacher who chose not to try with me or believe in me and who not only didn't celebrate my success but treated it like a fluke. Imagine what kind of hit that would have had on my self-esteem, my lack of faith in myself as a learner. Imagine if I didn't have a dad who could take the time or didn't have the knowledge to help me. Our schools are sadly filled with kids like that.

Being labeled as smart meant some of what I needed was also overlooked. Had I not been tested and selected for the G&T pilot program, would my struggles with spelling have been focused on in a positive, helpful way, or in a way that made me feel stupid? Labels can empower us or hinder us depending on the treatment and judgment associated with them. And for better or for worse, so much labeling takes place in our schools. Add to that the labels like dumb jock, theater nerd, band geek, etc. Lots of messages about who we are, that pigeonhole our skills, interests, and abilities, come to us in the hallowed halls of our learning environment.

What if at home we also hear messages like, "Your sister is the smart one, you're lazy, try harder." It's hard to try harder or do more when it doesn't make sense or come naturally to you. It's hard to try harder when you don't know how to access your resources or feel confident to speak up for yourself.

Many of the skills we need to succeed academically aren't specifically taught. Many of them come down to executive functioning—the area of our brain that impacts our ability to manage our emotions, regulate ourselves, manage time, plan, focus, and hold instructions in our working memory. Like everything, there is a spectrum of ability. Some people have impairments in executive functioning—like those with attention deficit disorders—and some kids just take time to learn and mature in this area.

Time management, organizational skills, note-taking, and study strategies are rarely explicitly taught. I was taught how to take notes based on the Carnegie method as a freshman in high school. I can't tell you how many people I have talked to who have said that no one ever showed them how to take notes. Instead of breaking down the help that we need, we are often blamed. We feel stupid or inadequate for not knowing how to help ourselves or do better. This is a tragedy because fear makes learning much more difficult.

It's why a negative school experience can have such a lasting impact. We feel vulnerable when we are learning something new. In the wrong setting, we can feel too vulnerable to share our ideas, thoughts, and feelings. On the other hand, too much stroking and reassurance can lead to an overestimation of our abilities. To where we become overly confident that we are indeed so smart because something came to us easily or we start to think we have nothing to learn.

As we've touched on in the last chapter, developing healthy self-esteem and being able to carry yourself with confidence doesn't come from being told everything you do is special and awesome, and amazing. Developing healthy self-esteem and being able to carry yourself with confidence comes from effort, evaluation, making mistakes, and learning to handle failure. It comes through learning, through study and application, and trial and error.

What we want is for students to try. We want them to be engaged. We want them to build on what they know and learn more. We want them to train their minds for thinking and discernment. We want them to discover the complexities and richness of the world. We want them to be curious. Rigidity stifles curiosity. Curiosity is what leads to discoveries. Curiosity is what keeps us learning outside the classroom and throughout life.

When we started our son at Shelton, we decided to have him repeat kindergarten and not be stretched too far. We wanted him to have the benefit of totally starting fresh with their structured, multi-sensory approach. For years, on the last day of school, he would feel sad knowing that his child-hood friends were moving on to the next grade—where he was once supposed to be. I can remember telling him what I was going to say was going to sound like such a mom thing, but to remember my words because one day, they would really and truly make sense to him. I told him that struggling in school was making him smarter, stronger, and more self-aware. I told him he was starting to understand his strengths and learning style in a way that many adults can't even begin to define for themselves. I told him his struggles would serve him well in the working world. I also shared with him some advice my aunt shared with me, that sometimes in life when things come too easily to people early on, they struggle later with how to handle setbacks.

GROWING OUR MINDSET

I marvel now that the TAG trend has been with us for many decades and how so many parents now want and expect their kids to be designated as gifted. Gifted has come to mean exceptional. And "on- level," oh dear, that is like being behind. Our culture of achievement is creating a type of dysmorphia. Like when I looked at the photos of my thighs and thought my body at its youthful prime was fat. And the problem with that is by fat, Doll, we mean flawed.

We all know that cultural standards for beauty shift and what was once unhealthy can become healthy. In an era where little girls compare themselves to Barbie doll figures and photoshopped images, our sense of normal body size is distorted. (I don't want to be too harsh on Barbie though, because I love her.) Likewise, in our culture of achievement, where only being exceptional is acceptable, then on-level, typical, or "normal" becomes not quite good enough.

I like to think we are all exceptional. Maybe not in the classroom, maybe not in Algebra, but we are all exceptional. It is our job to seek out and build upon what is exceptional in each of us. And we even get to be exceptional at more than one thing. We can be exceptional at our peak and then be not as good. We are allowed to shift. We are allowed to grow and change. It is even OK, to just be OK at something but still like it. Still feel good about that.

We have to guard against black and white thinking. That thin is equal to good or self-control. That making straight A's is equal to being intelligent and capable. Because if that is unequivocal, then fat is bad and Cs means you are stupid, less than. This is the curse of black and white thinking.

If what I believe is right, then if you believe differently, you must be wrong. It is the opposite of a growth mindset. A growth mindset says I may have a C but with guidance, tools, effort, and hard work I can get a B or even an A. A growth mindset means we can continue to learn, evolve, and improve. A growth mindset goes hand in hand with resilience. A growth mindset means you can learn and do and be anything you set your mind to.

Growing up, it was standard to grade on a curve that assumed an equal portion of kids must fail as those who excelled. Wouldn't the ideal goal of all learning be for every learner to master the content? In my mind, the bell curve is the perfect example of turning towards black and white thinking. It is fixed. A fixed mindset means things can't change. What was or is always must be. It is growth and change-resistant.

As a coach, I know and believe that people can change, learn, and adapt. It takes getting out of your comfort zone though. Those of us willing to adapt and learn new things get to do and experience more. Imagine the grandma who refuses to learn Zoom because using new technology makes her uncomfortable. She feels

Soft skills are the key to success in life.

like a fish out of water. How sad if she had missed out on connecting with her grandbabies during the pandemic because she was afraid to learn something new.

Learning is continuous. In life, we are not put in tracks determined by well-intentioned classroom management. We are not being graded in life. One of the biggest fallacies we are taught is that being an A student means you will be successful in life.

Soft skills are the key to success in life. We need education, don't get me wrong. We need hard skills and a working knowledge base. We need to learn how to learn. We need to know how to make connections between ideas and critical thinking skills. But how we navigate life, and our interpersonal skills, are far greater determinants of how successful we will be in life.

And the mother of all soft skills is communication. It's a skill that requires constant effort and refinement. But all other skills are rooted in our ability to express and share them. In my private coaching practice, and in the professional development classes I teach, I am constantly encouraging the development of our soft skills. The best classrooms, teachers, and coaches help us to foster our soft skills. But the good news is that we can study them and develop and improve them throughout our life.

One of my group coaching clients, a mom of a teenage son, shared a story after one of our sessions on communication skills. Her son was a Science, Technology, Engineering, and Math (STEM) star, and she attended a parent session at a STEM conference with her son. Each of the professors and business leaders on the panel gave their advice on what the kids should focus on for college and to have a successful career in STEM. Guess what every one of them said? Work on their communication skills. Boom.

Developing our soft skills and our emotional intelligence (EQ) is arguably more important than developing our academic skills. We need the mental powerhouse of those with high IQs, but we also need the builders, the connectors, and the communicators. And we need the creatives and visionaries who push the boundaries of learning and exploration. We need the people who ask "why?"

I am a big believer in classic college prep and liberal arts education because I do think that knowledge is power and learning how to express an opinion and argument is incredibly important. But I also believe too much emphasis has been placed on college as the path to success. Apprenticeship and on-the-job training for trades are thankfully making somewhat of a comeback. This shouldn't be seen as a fallback position, but an important, viable option for those wired for hands-on learning.

The good news in trying to prepare ourselves and our kids for the future is that we are no longer constrained by the halls of academia. The beautiful thing with the internet, tech, and now, the pandemic, is that there are so many new opportunities to learn. Books were one of the first things to unlock the world and allow people to visit different times and places in their minds. That was why people went to school—to have access to all that book learning and knowledge. Now we can see museums and travel from our laptops. We can watch "how-to" videos on YouTube and TikTok. Learning how to dance, speak a second language, or how to install a new toilet is now only a few clicks away. Virtually anything. Anything virtually. It is incredible. Imagine what Leonardo da Vinci would cook up now!

I haven't said enough about the arts, imagination, or travel. We know that little children learn through play, and we all learn through exploration. The multimedia options open doors for different learning styles. There are so many possibilities and that, Doll, is the goal of getting an education. To open doors, new horizons, new possibilities to tap into our potential. To learn, discover, grow, and evolve throughout our lives. To live and learn.

Lessons Learned

- Stay curious.
- Step out of your comfort zone.
- Learning isn't confined to four walls and one size does not fit all.
- It's OK to ask for help.
- Declare you are a lifelong learner, no matter what your major or career path.
- You miss out on the full spectrum of life with black and white thinking.
- We learn through struggle.
- We all have gifts and strengths and capabilities.
- "A for effort" is high honors—if you don't try you will never know what you are capable of achieving.
- EQ is as important as IQ.

Make it a Mantra (Repeat after me, Doll.)

- Growing and improving is within my control.
- I embrace everything that broadens my perspective and expands my thinking.
- Challenges are an opportunity for growth.
- I am a student of life and I enjoy learning.
- It feels good to feed my brain.
- I am smart, intelligent, and capable.
- I welcome challenges and face them with determination.
- I look forward to learning throughout my lifetime.
- I release old beliefs and labels that no longer serve me.
- I learn from my mistakes. I am always improving.
- Failure doesn't frighten me. I am brave enough to try.
- I step outside of my comfort zone with excitement and anticipation.
- My true potential is limitless.
- My curiosity and creativity lead me to new ideas and interesting places.
- I follow my muse.
- All things take effort. It will get easier. I will get better.
- I can always ask for help.
- I improve myself for myself.
- Learning opens doors and leads me to my future.
- I make time for creativity and exploration.

Powerful Questions

- What's your talent? What are you good at?
- How do you learn best?

- What is your next goal? Where do you want to go next, do next, learn next?
- What lesson do you wish you had learned sooner?
- What advice would you give your younger self?
- Is there an old story you have been telling yourself that is holding you back?
- How did a teacher or trusted adult help you to believe in yourself?
- What is something you always wanted to try? What's stopping you?
- How do you define being well-educated?
- What has taught you resilience? How are you developing a growth mindset?

Journal

_____

_____

_____

_____

_____

_____

_____

_____

_____

_____

_____

_____

_____

_____

_____

_____

_____

_____

_____

_____

_____

_____

Journal

_____

_____

_____

_____

_____

_____

_____

_____

_____

_____

_____

_____

_____

_____

_____

_____

_____

_____

_____

_____

_____

Journal

_____

_____

_____

_____

_____

_____

_____

_____

_____

_____

_____

_____

_____

_____

_____

_____

_____

_____

_____

Chapter 6

CAREER
LIFE IS NOT LINEAR

ONCE AGAIN, THE SOAP OPERAS GOT IT RIGHT! WE HAVE *One Life to Live*. And we live one life. Not a work life and a home life. Our jobs fund and fuel our lives, but they aren't our life. So, making your professional life and home life work together is incredibly important.

We've all heard the phrase work-life balance. It often feels impossible to give both parts of our life the attention they deserve. And if there is a crisis in one area or a major imbalance between the two, the other will be negatively impacted as well. If you are unhappy at work, I can just about guarantee you will be unhappy at home. We carry our stress with us. Sure, some people are better at compartmentalizing than others, but it takes a toll, and it always comes out one way or another.

Our new work from home normal of the pandemic highlighted the pros and cons of work-life separation or lack thereof. For my family, the pandemic provided an easier day with less time in the car, fewer early mornings, and actual time to talk to my husband at lunch. For others, of course, the pandemic created a strain with trying to juggle at-home learning and work, especially for those with younger children.

And, of course, many people have had to deal with professional shock waves. Furloughs, pay cuts, and job losses have taken their toll. As I write this, 2.4 million people have been out of work for 27 weeks or longer[13]. That is the threshold the U.S. Department of Labor uses to define long-term joblessness. So once again we are talking about the difference between a short-term crisis and a chronic situation.

During the onset of the pandemic, I had many women reaching out to me. Some had just started a job and been excited about it only to be abruptly laid off. Others had been laid off after many years at the same company. Finally, there were those that were either laid off or had their contract end right before the pandemic hit. For each of my clients who were in the position of having to look for work, they were naturally assessing their needs and criteria for the right job—the jobs that felt worth the energy it takes to even apply.

What came up repeatedly was the notion of working someplace where they would be excited to get out of bed and go to work, a place that felt worth the trade-offs in their personal lives. Now more than ever, people want to be much more selective about those tradeoffs. We've seen this with the younger generations entering the workforce and we are witnessing a concerning version of this with the number of women who left the workforce during the pandemic and now with the "Great Resignation"[14].

In September 2020, four times more women than men left the labor force in the United States[15]. Mothers faced with continuing to balance a workload, as well as family demands that felt untenable, chose to opt-out. The work-life balancing act, already an ongoing challenge for most of us, has hit a point of crisis for many mothers. The numbers tell us that mothers have thrown their hands up and said, we can't do it right now, it's not worth it, and that is concerning.

Job loss, like the other crises we've been exploring in this book, can cause us to question what we want out of our lives. Being out of a job can be terrifying and a major blow to our self-esteem, but once we get past the initial shock, it can be enlightening. Once again, we can take the time to examine which parts of our lives have been working well and which areas need adjusting. Having a break from the daily grind can provide the time and space we need to evaluate how our career reflects our goals and desires, and if it supports our bigger picture wants and needs. Does it reflect who we are and what we want?

Was the long commute killing you? Maybe that's something you won't compromise with the next job. Did you love working in a highly collaborative atmosphere? OK, great, that's something to look for and highlight in your job search. Would having more freedom and time with family be worth less responsibility and less money? Now may be the time to honor that. What trade-offs are your deal breakers? What are the things you cannot compromise on any longer? What compromises now seem worth it?

We change jobs for three reasons: dissatisfaction (we are no longer happy where we are or with what we are doing), need for more (more money, more responsibility, more recognition, more opportunity, growth, or new challenges,) or we leave involuntarily (fired, laid off, or furloughed). When we

You are much more than just your job title.

leave a job involuntarily, it can be particularly painful because we derive so much of our self-worth from our jobs.

Your position has been eliminated. You have been let go. You are no longer needed. Ouch. I get it, Doll. It hurts. It feels very personal. And while I don't ascribe to "it's not personal, it's business," the truth is you are not your job. It's hard not to suffer feelings of loss and failure. The feelings of accomplishment, productivity, and achievement that our professional lives offer can make it hard to separate our worth from our paycheck.

But no matter how much it stings, no matter how big a setback it might seem at the moment, you cannot let it undermine your confidence in the quality person that you are. You are much more than just your job title. And there will be other jobs.

REDIRECTION

One of my mantras is "It's not rejection, it's protection." It's helped me to process relationships as well as job changes. Others go with "It's not rejection, it's redirection." That works too. What I have learned is that it truly always is one or the other. So don't be paralyzed by the prospect of unexpected, or what may at first seem like unwelcome change. Involuntary job loss can serve as a course correction.

I will never forget hearing from a mutual friend and past colleague about a person I had to fire. He told her it was the best thing that ever happened to him! It is never fun to have to let someone go. The only thing worse is being the one let go. It's incredibly stressful to fire someone even when you know it is the right course of action. Still, hearing his feedback was validating and such a relief. He was miserable and it showed. It was only after he was fired that he could be totally honest with himself about that. Once in the right line of work, he was flourishing and succeeding, and was eventually promoted into management!

Why do we stay in jobs when all the signs point to the fact that it's a bad fit? Well, I would argue it's primarily inertia. It's also because looking for a job is hard. It takes a lot of time and energy. You have to put yourself out there. That can be uncomfortable and staying even when you are miserable can seem easier. We fear change. We fear rejection.

Often, we stay because we're unhappy but not completely miserable yet. We might like some things but not others. Maybe what was once a good match is no longer a fit. Management has changed, your needs have changed, maybe it was never that great, but you were making it work because you liked the clients, or your coworkers, or the money was good. Whatever the case, I once again urge you to listen to the whispers before it turns into not being able to take it another day, or worse, the choice is made for you.

Some of the whispers and signs of inertia are boredom, lack of focus, and procrastination. They are the more niggling feelings and signs that it's probably time to move on or to get proactive in your current role and seek added experience and challenges. Procrastination gets a bad rap for obvious reasons, but it can be a valuable teacher if you get down to the emotion underneath the procrastination. Do you hate the task

The "we're no longer whispering and starting to shout now" signs mean you have moved into the danger zone of burnout.

or fear it's too hard? Do you feel overwhelmed by it or ill-equipped? What is holding you back? What is the root cause?

The "we're no longer whispering and starting to shout now" signs mean you have moved into the danger zone of burnout. The kind of burnout that goes beyond, "I need a break," or "I need a vacation," is destructive. It's putting stress into the chronic column, and by now if anything is clear, it's that we're trying to mitigate and avoid as many chronic challenges as we can, Doll.

Cynicism, interpersonal conflict, physical, mental, and emotional exhaustion. You can't sleep, you can't think, you can't get anything done. You don't want to get out of bed. You don't want to do anything when it comes to work. It's more than procrastination, it's like how I felt when my thyroid gave up, you just can't dig up any more energy to put toward your job.

Or when you do, you find yourself on edge, anxious, frustrated, or angry. That is burnout that has already wound its way into your core. You must deal with it before you begin to feel that you have no choice but to quit or leave before you are 100% sure or ready.

Sorting all this out requires honesty. You have to take a hard look at who you are, where you are, what you are doing, who you are doing it with and the boundaries you are holding or not holding with meeting all your needs. Sometimes we tip over into burnout not because of what is demanded of us, but because of what we demand of ourselves. Either way, burnout is like the base falling out of the pyramid. The house of cards comes crashing down.

OUR NEEDS ARE REAL

You have probably heard of Maslow's Hierarchy of Needs[16]. Self-actualization is at the top of the pyramid—the pinnacle if you will. And that's quite apropos when we think of professional success. We even call it that. "They've reached the pinnacle of their career." The pinnacle of success.

SELF-ACTUALIZATION
SELF-ESTEEM
LOVE AND BELONGING
SAFETY AND SECURITY
PHYSIOLOGICAL NEEDS

Self-actualization is the desire to become the most that one can be. Right before we reach self-actualization, we have esteem, love and belonging, safety, and physiological needs. They break down as follows:

*   Esteem—respect, self-esteem, status, recognition, strength, freedom.
*   Below that are Love and Belonging—friendship, intimacy, family, sense of connection.
*   Then we have Safety needs—personal security, employment, resources, health, property.

- At the base of the pyramid are Physiological needs—our most basic requirements to live—air, water, food, shelter, sleep, clothing, reproduction.

When I said that work funds and fuels our lives, this is what I mean. A job, a means to provide for our basic needs, is essential. It funds our ability to live. When we move from a job where we punch the clock and make some money, to a true professional calling, this is usually how we differentiate the idea of a career versus a bunch of jobs strung together. A career bridges and propels us to the top of Maslow's Hierarchy of Needs. Respect, status, recognition, those can come from other places culturally, like family, for example. But our careers are so often an essential part of having esteem. What we typically dream of, are careers like a famous person or our heroes, of people who appear to be self-actualized. That person who embodies their talents fully. It's hard to imagine becoming the most that someone can be without that professional piece in place where their true talents and passions shine.

When we pursue the pinnacle and start to forget about the foundational levels that supported us in reaching the top of our game, we get into big trouble. This is the burnout of perfectionists, of over-achievers, the people-pleasers, and the ol' Type A personality. You must still meet those foundational level needs, or the base starts to erode and the whole pyramid comes tumbling down.

I am always reminding people that it's incredibly important to proactively manage your career. The sooner you adapt your mindset to the fact that companies own jobs, and you own your career, the sooner you will invest in your professional development, and be more attuned to opportunities. A well-managed career provides the work that goes beyond just funding your life into fueling your life. A well-managed, intentional career allows you to reach the pinnacle of self-actualization, but it must always be part of a well-managed life, where all your needs are supported and met.

While we admire people who have enormous professional success, we also can think of many cautionary tales of famous folks who had incredibly sad personal lives. I don't think you can fully be "the most of who you are" without understanding your essence, who you are at your core. When we aren't clear about who we are, it is easy to take step after step down a career and life path that isn't right for us. Many of us don't realize it until we've gotten lost or at least taken a few wrong turns.

There is a saying nowadays that there is no longer a career ladder as much as there is a career jungle gym. Many of us though still have the progressive career ladder embedded deep in our brains. As with education, for a long time, we were collectively conditioned to think of our careers as progressing linearly, taking one step up the ladder to GET TO THE TOP! To be a manager. An owner. The boss. To climb higher and higher. Some people were so ingrained in this thinking that they saw it as OK to step on people to get to the top. Winning and achieving were worth it. Beating the competition necessitated it.

But what's that other saying? "It's lonely at the top." It's lonely at the top if you have to make hard decisions alone and in a vacuum. It's lonely at the top if you've crushed others to get there. It's lonely at the top if you have no one to celebrate and share your success with. It's lonely at the top if you don't have the time or energy to even enjoy your own company. It's lonely at the top if someone is trying to knock you off your perch to take your place because you have both dedicated your lives to thinking there's only room for one up there.

As I discussed in previous chapters; it is important to explore your definition of success early on. What does success look like to you? Your definition may not be the same as mine. Your definition may not be the same as your parents'. It might not be the same as your partner's (which I hate to tell you may be a problem).

Is it defined in dollars or life balance? Do you value time over money? People over material things? What does professional success look like to you? How does that marry with being a successful person, parent, or partner? And how does your definition of success line up with your values? Is it compatible with who you are at your core? Can you reach the true pinnacle of self-actualization if what you do is at odds with who you are, with your spirit, your essence?

How can you know you have succeeded if you don't know how it will be measured? Will you ever feel successful if you are using an old yardstick? Someone else's yardstick? And further, how can you determine the right career path if you aren't clear on what you truly want out of life?

I loved sales, but I couldn't and didn't thrive in just any sales environment. I could not sell a product I didn't believe in deeply, and I couldn't sell in an environment where people gamed the system and fudged the numbers. I am competitive and goal-oriented, but I learned the hard way that working collaboratively is essential to me. Being in a leadership role that still allows time for my family is also fundamental to who I am. For me, that's not worth compromising for even a few years.

Others may choose careers that require great personal sacrifice, but it speaks to their core and their dreams of an ideal life. Defining success and a life well-lived is highly personal. Understanding what we are looking for from our work, in terms of self-actualization, is fundamental to building our pyramids and maintaining a solid foundation.

Understanding who we are at our essence is fundamental to making smart career choices. When we make the wrong move, we tend to explain it away with a common phrase, "it wasn't the right fit." We've all heard it said. "It was a bad fit." I always picture people squirming when I hear this phrase, trying to pull off a sweater two sizes too small. or loosening their tie like they can't breathe. Or worse, trying to get in and out of a sports bra!

What does it mean when a job's a bad fit? So often it has very little to do with the actual work—although that can be the case. More often, it comes down to personality style, work environment, and values—who someone is at their core. When it is a case of a mismatch with the actual work, that speaks to interests, skills, and strengths. This does matter. Greatly. People who use their strengths daily are six times more engaged at work[17]. Why? Because they enjoy it more and feel good about themselves. Our strengths are an essential part of who we are. They help to define us.

When clients come to me looking for a career change, or when I am working with a young person who is just starting, we start by exploring and naming their strengths and transferable skills and exploring their interests. It's fascinating when I do my favorite career assessment with older workers who have gone through some twists and turns. The interests that get represented in their profile reports, inevitably are validated by past jobs, courses they loved in college, or their hobbies. It gives me such confidence when I can use this for younger folks. Following your interests, and the path that workers who share your interests have taken can lead to fulfilling careers.

When it comes to making career choices, you will hear purpose and passion come up all the time. "Find your purpose." "Follow your passion." Sometimes, the two concepts are used almost interchangeably. Deep down, most people desire to live a life of purpose, on purpose. But finding our true purpose often takes time and feels harder than we expect it should. It's the other reason why careers are more like jungle gyms!

Deep down, most people desire to live a life of purpose, on purpose.

Purpose, as I mentioned, is sometimes talked about as passion. "Do what you love, and the money will follow." I believe this, but only when you are realistic that even when you are doing what you love you won't love it all the time. And that not everything you love will be the right career choice. Expectations are everything!

Focusing on our interests can help us find our passion while naming and defining our innate strengths and our skill sets will help us take our interests and our passions and turn them into purpose. Once we know that, then we need to look at our personality. How we communicate, our environmental preferences, etc. Because our personality and our values are what will determine where we are the best fit.

Just like a company has its core values, so do each of us. Many of us haven't taken the time to sit down and define them. We kind of know them, but if I put you on the spot could you list them? I want you to be able to. It's so important when determining either what employer you want to work for or defining who you want to be as a business owner. Values are also the cornerstone when it comes to work-life balance.

Whether you are just starting, making a career change, rejoining the workforce, or looking for a new job in the same industry, all these pieces are the same. You need to be clear on who you are and how to position and sell yourself. This is the personal branding you hear so much about.

I have a friend who is a tax accountant. For many, that does not check the box when we think of "finding your passion." When we talk about passion, it sounds like it should be something extraordinary, and crunching numbers doesn't sound glamourous or special. To many, it would be tedious or taxing (no pun intended), but for her, it works. She likes it.

She's problem-solving and helping people find ways to protect themselves and save money. She works with a wide variety of clients in her small town and beyond. She likes working with numbers and she's good at it. Doing something you are good at feels good. That should not be underestimated. She also makes good money doing it. Also, not to be underestimated!

Her personality style is analytical, conscientious, and task-oriented, followed by people-oriented, supportive, team-player tendencies. You can see where her innate personality is also well-suited for her work.

My friend also writes and officiates weddings in her spare time. It feeds an entirely different side of her. I do not doubt that she will release a novel one day, but I think she'll always be crunching numbers because it works. Literally. It funds and fuels her life in a way that excites her brain so that she is satisfied with her work. It allows her to take care of her family in a way that officiating weddings probably never could. Do you see how it all comes together?

YOUR REASON FOR BEING

This brings us to the concept of Ikigai. If you cannot be paid for your passion, then it probably isn't a viable vocation. At least not in the short run. Ikigai is a Japanese concept which in English translates to "our reason for being"—our purpose[18]. It helps us understand that what we are most meant to be doing with our lives can be found at the intersection of doing what we love (interests), doing what we are good at (strengths/skills), doing something the world needs, and doing something others will pay us for. This is the sweet spot. This is the difference between passion and purpose. This is the difference between a job and a career.

If you are doing something the world needs and you love doing it, you might feel you are living your mission. You might feel good and happy about that, but you may not be able to eat. If you are doing something you love and are good at it, again you may feel you are exploring your passion and be very fulfilled and thrilled doing it, but you may not feel useful. It may not provide the practical things you need. (Remember the base of the pyramid?)

If you are doing something you can be paid for and you are good at it, you are making a living and might be comfortable but not fulfilled (the top of the pyramid). If you are getting paid and doing something the world needs, that may be exciting but can lead to complacency and even insecurity. What do you do if the world stops wanting what you are doing?

Using the Ikigai model for finding your purpose (your reason for being) can help you identify where you are right now and why you feel stuck and how to find the balance and fulfillment you are seeking. That feeling of being stuck is the emotional signpost that says it's time to move. You have to meet this emotion with radical honesty so you can make a good assessment of which direction to move in, and which path you need to take to get there.

Sometimes this is just a simple crossroads where you take on a new project, lighten your workload, or a little more significant change, like switching roles within an organization or moving to a new company. Other times that feeling of being stuck is a sign that it's time to reinvent yourself. Either way, using a SWOT analysis can be a great tool to pair with the Ikigai model. Taking a hard look at your Strengths, Weaknesses, Opportunities, and Threats (potential challenges, missing skills, or deficits) means treating your career like a business. And that is exactly how you should be managing it.

Again, we want to ensure that our work life is in keeping with our bigger picture life goals and who we are at our core. Once you've decided on the path you are going to take, you need to quality-check your choice with your core values. Our core values are our compass. Ensure that you are on the right path by double-checking your compass. You will likely never feel fulfilled if you are working in a job that goes against either your innate personality or your values.

That said, once you are clear, leap. Don't be afraid because the whole path isn't clear, if you are stepping out with clarity about who you are and are guided by your values, you can step into the future with confidence. And that's the beautiful thing, the more intentional you are about managing your career, the more attuned you will be to opportunities. Coming to new crossroads will be exciting, and unexpected travelers will appear, and new routes will start to open up.

It's easier to take those leaps of faith when you are confident in your self-knowledge. Don't stay stuck. No one can keep you in a dead-end job. Backtrack your way out if you must, but only you can keep yourself stuck in place.

I hope you find that looking at your career this way is empowering. That you aren't stuck on some rung of a corporate ladder, or the career jungle gym because you can make the next move. Laterally, back down or up and over. There are lots of ways to the top. You are in control.

Most importantly, you are in control of your mindset. I know some of you jumped off the jungle gym and climbing back on is intimidating. But you know how to play on the playground. It may have changed a little, but the basics are still the same. You are allowed to play. You are capable of climbing. You belong. Do not let fear hold you back.

For those that were let go, maybe you had hit a low point and were no longer effective. Even if you were ineffective, it does not mean that you are defective. You are not your job, so don't beat yourself up, but do start with radical honesty and self-awareness.

Break down what worked well and what you could do differently. What fit your needs and what didn't? Take a step back and find the lessons. Go back to the SWOT analysis. Go back to the Ikigai model. Look at the other areas of life outside of work where your interests, skills, and talents manifest themselves. Previous jobs, education, volunteer, civic, hobbies, and leisure activities. Start to follow the breadcrumbs and soon your path will begin to become clear, you will no longer feel lost. Your confidence and excitement will come back.

And while I'm swinging between the playground and hiking metaphors, let's step off the path and come back to the playground. This time the seesaw. If your crisis and confusion are coming from bouncing back and forth between prioritizing work and dropping the ball at home and then smack back to the opposite, then you are on the work-life seesaw, and honestly, the seesaw was never that much fun. It got old fast.

If work is on one side and life is on the other, then the balance is the fulcrum in the middle. It's the pivot point. When you tip too far to one side and people start bouncing off or landing too hard, you know it's time to push back. The important thing to note is that the fulcrum doesn't move. It is unchanging—stable. Another definition for the word fulcrum, according to the Oxford dictionary, is a thing that plays a central or *essential* role in an activity, event, or situation. Our core, our compass, our values are the fulcrum.

When we focus on the fulcrum and stay aligned with it, the seesaw stays balanced. Our core values are both what center and guide us back to the center. Back into alignment. So, if you are feeling out of alignment, you must take a hard look at your values and how they are being expressed. Look at the choices you need to make and how you need to adjust, and it will become clear how to pivot. Only then will you be back on the right path and feeling more balanced and in control of your career.

Lessons Learned

◆ Work funds and fuels our life—it's not our whole life.

◆ You are more than a job title.

◆ Companies own jobs; you own your career.

◆ When we focus on our values it is easier to find balance.

◆ Success is subjective.

◆ Our interests pave our career paths.

◆ A dead-end is just a U-turn.

◆ Shore up your foundation.

◆ The only person capable of holding you back is you. If you're stuck, don't stay there.

◆ When you are in tune with yourself and your goals, you will be more attuned to opportunities.

Make it a Mantra (Repeat after me, Doll.)

◆ I have the grit to accomplish my goals.

◆ I can. I will. I am capable and worthy.

◆ I am responsible for my future.

◆ I have what it takes—I will succeed.

◆ The world needs my unique brand of skills, talents, experience, and perspective.

◆ Working hard with purpose and intent brings me closer to my goals.

◆ I am attracting the support I need to achieve even greater things.

◆ I have unlimited potential.

◆ My dreams are coming true.

◆ I am attuned to new opportunities.

◆ I am building a career that supports a life that I love.

- I know who I am and what I want to do.
- I have clarity about my purpose and gifts and confidently share who I am and what I want with others.
- I am focused and confident and motivated to make my mark.
- I am excited about the future I am creating.
- I am a star in my field.
- I work with driven team players; we bring out the best in each other.
- I am appreciated and valued for my contributions.
- I will know when to make my next move.
- I use my time and talents wisely.
- I am clear on what steps to take in my professional journey.

Powerful Questions

- What is it you love to do?
- What did you want to do when you were little?
- How are your values represented in your work?
- Does your job support your larger life goals?
- Do you have a short, medium, and long-term plan to reach your career goals?
- How do you define success?
- Why do you work?
- What is the worst thing that has happened to you professionally, and what did you learn from it?
- What would a better work-life balance look like to you?
- Procrastination, avoidance, boredom, and burnout are messengers—what are they telling you?

Journal

_____

_____

_____

_____

_____

_____

_____

_____

_____

_____

_____

_____

_____

_____

_____

_____

_____

_____

_____

_____

_____

_____

Journal

Journal

Chapter 7

LEADERSHIP
STEP UP AND STAND OUT

THERE'S NEVER BEEN A TIME IN ALL OF HUMANITY WHEN WE didn't need leaders and leadership. We have many lessons on power, authority, and the ability to inspire, persuade, and impact others—from the classic treatises and tales from antiquity to what's trending on social media today.

If you were to Google quotes on leadership, you'd be just as likely to find something that resonates from Marcus Aurelius as you would Eleanor Roosevelt or Oprah Winfrey. We have many examples to learn from and lessons that seem destined to repeat themselves. Understanding others and being able to motivate and persuade them is critically important if you want to be able to get things done.

How a leader handles themself during unexpected challenges is critical. A crisis can make or break a leader. Our global pandemic has underscored how leadership and crisis management are intertwined. From the president to the local school principal, there were, and are, hard decisions to be made.

While my career has taken a winding path to bring me to where I am today, I still take many lessons from what I learned as a political science major. You can't explore how societies are governed without exploring leadership on every level of society. In our homes, in our classrooms, in our boardrooms, and, of course, in the public sector, too, we need leaders. Strong, effective, inspiring, impactful, visionary, supportive, conscientious, harmonizing, calculating leadership.

When we think of the personal changes, challenges, and crises we face, it may be hard to think in the context of leadership. But how many times have we heard the phrase "a failure of leadership?" Failures of leadership may well impact your life, particularly professionally. It is well documented that people don't leave jobs, they leave managers[19]. They leave uninspiring, unsupportive, ineffective, hostile, or incompetent leaders.

We are called to assess the leadership qualities of others and often we are called to lead from right where we are, ready or not. Life requires us to be discerning, to make hard choices, to stay true to our values and beliefs. To do the right thing and to be ethical and moral. To think of others as well as ourselves. To step up and to take a stand.

Whether it's for the PTA, our company as a member of a team, or as the head of our household, we are called to show up with intention and with purpose. When we think of the self-actualization pinnacle level of Maslow's Hierarchy of Needs, we realize there is a component of leadership within it. We can't be fully self-actualized sitting on the sidelines of life. We have to show up. You can't be a leader in any sense of the word if you don't show up. In order to step up and stand out you have to show up—over and over—as your best self.

For our purposes, Doll, let's focus on the idea of personal power even when we may feel out of control with what is happening in the larger world around us. As I said at the beginning, it all comes down to you. You have to take the reins

You can't be a leader in any sense of the word if you don't show up.

of your own life. You have to decide who you want to be and lead yourself towards her as you show up every day and invest in growing yourself towards your highest, shiniest, fully actualized self.

Leadership means taking responsibility and control. It means firmly owning that "the buck stops" with you and accepting the consequences of your actions, then dealing with them, especially when things don't go as planned. Leaders have the guts to keep going when the chips are down. They find creative solutions to their problems. They learn from their mistakes when things don't go as planned. And leaders see possibility when others see only obstacles or a lack of options. When others see nothing but white space on a blank canvas, leaders see possibility. And then they set about creating.

In any crisis, your leadership skills will help you move forward because leaders tackle their goals and face their problems with tenacity and grit. When I think of all the different characteristics and aspects of leadership, what strikes me most is this idea of creating and creative problem-solving. And creation—creation—wow—that holds the energy of the future—of forward movement.

As leaders, we help ourselves and others move forward. We lead the charge onward and upward. So, when you are stuck or face a setback in life, and need to draw on your inner leader, what does she look like?

Packaged within our innate personalities are our natural leadership styles. This is the source of our power. We've talked about self-awareness and understanding our personality style, especially when we explored our relationships and communication skills in chapter two, and also in thinking about our education and careers. This is where our emotional intelligence and soft skills come in once again. To quote leadership theorist and author, John Adair, "Communication is the sister of leadership."

You will not be an effective leader of others if you are not an effective communicator. And you will struggle to motivate, persuade, and inspire others if you don't understand what makes them tick. So, our interpersonal skills and our emotional intelligence are what set us apart as leaders. Our soft skills are the keys to success for each of us no matter what we do, but if you want to stand out from the crowd, then yours need to be next level.

STEP INTO YOUR SUPERPOWER

The best leaders adapt and adopt from other styles to fit the needs of the other person and the moment, but they are clear on how to tap into their own strengths—their unique superpowers. True leaders step into their power so they can step out, step up, and stride forward. They own it.

A supportive (high S) personality who is a natural-born servant leader, for example, won't be authentic trying to drive

156

people with an authoritarian style like dominant (high D) personality. They may need to adopt traits of a dominant style leader to take charge from time to time, but their strength will be in motivating others while working alongside them in a supportive, nurturing way. (If you haven't read chapter two yet, go read it now.)

Again, this is just a basic overview of one's highest trait. Your unique personality blend will further influence your source of strength and leadership style. That is why I always say that success begins with self-awareness. It's true for success in any of the areas of our lives that we have been exploring but more so when we think of leadership.

The best leaders are self-aware. They know themselves and they continually review, assess, and strive to improve themselves. Leaders who level out, peter out, flame out, or worse, get thrown out, have often lost their way due to a lack of awareness. It may be that they are surrounded by sycophants or are so used to pushing past resistance that they have mistakenly underestimated it.

And listen, Doll, I'm not trying to suggest failure is always our fault. Bad things happen to good people. There are things that we have no control over. Even the best leaders can be put in situations that are stacked against them. But we want to be proactive, pay attention, and control what we can.

Lean into your strengths, your superpowers, but use them for your good and the good of others. That tenet will most times keep you from steering off course. But also keep your powers under control. Think about the superheroes from comic books and movies. They have remarkable powers, but they understand the repercussions of using them. Instead, they use them discerningly and control them. They are aware

Strengths excessively relied upon can become weaknesses.

of their weaknesses too—their kryptonite—and they seek to avoid them.

Evil villains do the opposite, don't they? They find their power and maximize and push it to its limit and use it almost exclusively. They are so overconfident in their powers that they think they can't fail. They believe winning is assured because they are so over-confident in the rarity and specialness of their super strength. But it always ends in negative outcomes and destruction.

Strengths excessively relied upon can become weaknesses. Beware of the blind spots you may have about yourself. Beware of overused go-to abilities that may have gotten you where you are but might be now spinning out of control. Overused strengths can stunt your continued growth, cloud your judgment, or cause you to overplay your hand when making the bold and hard choices that leadership requires of us.

This is why the best leaders surround themselves with people who have other skills and strengths that balance and enhance their capabilities. The best leaders recognize their limitations and aren't afraid of other people's superpowers. They remain confident in their abilities and continue to strength-train but have clarity and an accurate perception of themselves.

Here's the other thing we can learn from the stories of superheroes—they empower themselves. They discover a talent or strength within themselves, and they explore it. They nurture and develop it. They get *curious* about it. And they follow that curiosity through to creation—of a new, better, more incredible, more powerful version of themselves. Then they build on the strength and refine it. And what does that do? It opens up a whole new world for them. New opportunities, new challenges.

Our superheroes don't wait for permission from someone else to say, "Hey, what new strengths have you discovered lately?" They empower themselves. They empower themselves by simply going where their power and curiosity lead them. They give themselves permission to explore, develop, and try. They don't wait for permission from someone else to start testing their new strengths and budding confidence.

In the typical superhero genesis story, they don't even have all these new powers figured out before they start to test them. They stumble upon some strengths, others they discover through answering the question "I wonder if I could ...." They fail forward. In business, this is the key to innovation. It's the same for personal development. When we fail forward, we test our limits and build our confidence in our capabilities. We learn in real-time by leaps and bounds.

So, what are you waiting for? Permission? From whom? The commissioner? You have to empower yourself, Doll. Ask yourself, "What if I could ...?" Step into your superpower. Fail forward. Try. Test. Learn. Leap!

LEAD FROM WHERE YOU ARE

You don't have to be a superhero or CEO to be a leader. A leader is someone whom others look up to. A leader is someone who is self-possessed and capable of keeping their own counsel. This doesn't mean they don't have mentors or don't seek a sounding board when making decisions, but they have confidence in themselves and their choices.

While it's important to keep our ego in check, a crisis of confidence is probably the worst thing that can happen to us as leaders. Bosses, business owners, frankly anyone who's ever chaired an auction, has probably hit this low point. A crisis of confidence is when you are standing at the edge of the abyss. You are overwhelmed, unsure, and are positive this is not what you signed up for! You can't go on. You're finished. But as the leader and the one in charge, you are left holding the bag. If you don't go on, how will anyone else?

Holding on when you are feeling untethered requires radical resilience. These are the times when you have to dig deeper into the toolbox. Finding and utilizing your resources is one important way to regain your grip. Everyone needs their own board of directors—that A-list group of people with experience and wisdom that can lend perspective and strength. We need mentors, advisors, and coaches. The best of the best build this network and create it when they don't have it. They pay, if necessary, for the expertise that they need, whether that's a trainer or a therapist, a consultant or a concierge. Wise leaders know when to find and ask for the help they need.

And wise leaders move beyond the idea of perfection. Not just in the sense of failing forward, but with the awareness that others don't expect perfection from them. News flash, Doll, most people are already quite clear that you're not perfect, but they like and admire and believe in you anyway. They will still work hard for and with you and stand by and with you. Thinking we have to do it all and be it all can be a major contributor to a crisis of confidence when faced with major setbacks and obstacles.

Ultimately trying to be it all and do it all by yourself isn't leading and certainly, you can never scale in a significant way if you remain the one trying to hold on to all the control. This is what we talked about in parenting when

Trying to control everything is a form of fear.

we discussed letting go so our kids can come into their own. The same is true in the workplace. If you don't believe anyone else can do it as well as you and you don't know how to train, coach, mentor, motivate, inspire, or flat-out direct others and delegate to get the results you desire, then you can't grow as an organization.

Trying to control everything is a form of fear. It can come from the desire to get known results; to ensure the quality work you are known for, for example. But control requires us to hold on tight and we can't reach up and keep climbing if we are holding on. So, leadership also requires trust and faith not just in ourselves but in others. The good news is that the skills we need to manage others can also be learned and developed.

CONFIDENCE AND CAPABILITY

A crisis of confidence can come when you are tested from outside yourself, but it can also be an internal battle. The most talked-about form of this phenomenon is imposter syndrome, where you feel like a fake. That feeling that someone will discover that you aren't who you say you are because you aren't all that. It's the fear that others will realize you aren't talented enough, qualified enough, experienced enough, smart enough, or good enough. The fear you will be found out.

This can be hard when you are testing out new strengths (or dusting off old ones) and aren't completely sure of yourself. You haven't proven yourself, so the level of belief in your abilities is hard to hold onto. From both my coaching and personal experience, I know that many moms who re-enter the workplace struggle deeply with this, although they are certainly not the only ones.

Remember our superheroes? They defined who they were and would be based on what they knew to be true about their character, strengths, and skills. They crafted that costume and chose the emblem emblazoned on their chest. They chose their brand, built it, and embodied it before anyone knew who the hell they were. Is that a bird? Is that a plane? No, it's me, a badass. They envisioned it. You have to do the same, Doll. Envision it and then embody it.

The fear is real and sometimes even superheroes get their asses kicked. You will also be shown to be fallible, imperfect, and no matter what, some people will still think you aren't all that. There are Marvel people, and there are DC people. You will be criticized fairly and unfairly. You may get a smackdown. And when this happens you will lick your wounds, train, and put the suit back on. You will keep showing up. You will deal with it, Doll, like the powerful *wonder*ful woman you are.

And this is honestly the myth of greatness—the kind of greatness we expect in leaders in their field. We compare ourselves against them and see perfection—the pinnacle. We marvel at their accomplishments as if they somehow came easily to them. Even those with great natural gifts practiced and worked to get where they are, and they made mistakes along the way.

We expect to be great out of the gate. Behind the stories of overnight successes that we often admire, are tales of incredible perseverance, self-belief, desire, and determination. These phenoms chose to believe in themselves when others didn't believe in them, and they practiced. So much practice.

What we can learn from the superstars and top athletes is the power of manifesting our dreams. You've heard of the world-class sprinters who envision embodying the cheetah, the Olympic swimmers who go over every stroke in their mind again and again. They are using the power of visioning. Rather than give in to anxiety and fear, they use the power of their mind to create a self-fulfilling prophecy of success. They practice success in their head. They rehearse the steps they need to take. They envision success. They smell it, they taste it, and they feel it. They see the platinum album on the wall. They practiced their acceptance speech for the Oscars when they were still auditioning for their big break.

We can practice what we want our outcomes to look like too. We can imagine the hard conversations and practice our perfect presentations. We can see ourselves where we want to be—leading with confidence and authority. Winning, creating, building, thriving.

The more you envision the event with your whole body and with all your senses, the more real it becomes in your mind, and the more powerful the programming you are uploading into your conscious mind and the subconscious as well. Run that tape over and over and shut out fear, which is the real imposter, and embody your boldest, baddest, most amazing super self.

Lessons Learned

- Success begins with self-awareness.
- You can't evolve if you can't adapt.
- Leaders amplify and empower others. Empowered people empower people.
- Lead where you are.
- Stay true to your style and your superpowers.
- Obstacles are opportunities.
- Build your own brand—leave a legacy.
- You can't be a good leader if you are not a good communicator.
- Fail forward. Leap.
- Strengths over-relied upon can become weaknesses.

Make it a Mantra (Repeat after me, Doll.)

- I believe in myself.
- I surround myself with smart, resourceful people who make me better.
- My focus is sharp, clear, and conscious. I let go of all distractions.
- I am ready. I have prepared for this.
- I bring out the best in myself and others.
- I have the discipline to stay focused on the things I want to accomplish.
- Others look to me for guidance.
- Courage flows through me.
- No matter what obstacles are put in front of me, I will rise to the challenge.
- I am building mutually beneficial connections.

- I am calm under pressure and can handle whatever comes my way.
- I see creative solutions and new opportunities.
- I adapt quickly and instinctively know what each situation requires of me.
- I drive results and make things happen.
- I am inspired and inspire others.
- I am steady and supportive.
- I deliver quality and excellence consistently.
- I have earned the respect of those I work with and treat others with the respect they deserve.
- I carry myself with poise and confidence.
- I am intentional in all I do.

Powerful Questions

- Do you celebrate the success of others or struggle with feelings of jealousy?
- What leadership qualities do you admire?
- Have you ever failed as a leader? What did you learn and how did you overcome the situation?
- Who or what intimidates you and why?
- Have you struggled with imposter syndrome?
- Envision your dream accomplishment. Describe it in detail. How can you begin to embody this vision?
- What strength might you be over-relying upon? How can you balance and develop your other strengths as a leader?
- Have you had to make a difficult decision where others didn't agree with your approach, direction, or decision? What did you learn? Would you do it again?

+ Are you standing in the full truth of your superpowers?
+ What is your personal brand? What are you known for? When do others seek you out?
+ How do you empower those around you?

Journal

Journal

Journal

_____

_____

_____

_____

_____

_____

_____

_____

_____

_____

_____

_____

_____

_____

_____

_____

_____

_____

_____

Chapter 8

WEALTH
THE BOTTOM LINE

I STARTED THIS BOOK FOCUSED ON HEALTH AND WE'RE ENDING with wealth. It feels like the perfect bookends for the pandemic which birthed this work.

What comes to mind when you hear the word wealth, Doll? Being rich? Money? Affluence? Prosperity? Abundance?

Like deciding what is essential to each of us, like defining what success means to me versus you, we have to determine what wealth means to each of us.

For me, wealth, or prosperity, encompasses so much more than just finances. And interestingly, the Old English meaning of wealth was welfare and well-being.[20] Health and wealth. Bookends to wholeness.

We had a real chicken and the egg argument in our country, and across the world, when our health and safety became diametrically opposed to our ability to work. We debated which should be the priority. Shut down to stay healthy and lose your customers, your business, your income? Or stay open, keep the economy churning, and possibly lose a few days, weeks, or months of your life to illness?

Keeping people home so they didn't get sick, but not being able to keep the economy open led to job loss and decreases in income which led to stress, food insecurity, and fear. But of course, as the virus ravaged so many, we were also reminded that we can't work if we are ill, let alone dead.

We saw people panicking at the beginning and trying to hoard resources. They wanted to ensure they could take care of themselves and their families. We were afraid of going without.

Humans have always had to endure times of hardship and scarcity. Plagues, famines, war, natural and man-made disasters. Fear of scarcity or lack lives deep in our collective consciousness. Many my age and older had grandparents who lived through the Great Depression. And I think about the word depression when we look at the link between health and wealth, between our ability (or inability) to support ourselves financially, and the impact that has on our well-being.

Many experiences shape our opinions on wealth and how fortunate we are (or aren't) and our relationship with money. Many of our subconscious feelings and collective stories around wealth have surfaced with the pandemic. It's wrong to hoard (It's selfish and greedy, we shouldn't be miserly, right Tiny Tim?) Every man for himself (Others are selfish and greedy, so don't be a sucker. Take what's yours. I'm going to protect what's mine.) Even tribalism has reemerged locally and internationally (from travel restrictions to no outsiders in certain communities or crossing of borders).

Tribalism is self-protective and rooted in family and the impulse to take care of your own to ensure survival. Are we to be applauded for our survival instincts or chastised for letting our lizard brains take over? In survival mode, we are at the base of Maslow's Hierarchy of Needs. We have a fear of lack. We aren't likely to think of the big picture or long-term. But it's real. Those are after all our most basic needs.

What do deprivation and lack do to us? A depressed economy can lead to a depressed people.

STAYING WHOLE

When I did the Eurail thing after my semester abroad in Spain, I visited Prague, Czechoslovakia. It was just after the Velvet Revolution and before the country split into two sovereign states. It was such a sharp contrast to the other bustling cities we had hit along the way. The feeling of lack was palpable. Everyone was dressed in dark, dull colors. No one looked at anyone else on the metro. It felt like Burgermeister Meisterburger[21] ruled the town. There were very few tourists, and shops were mostly empty.

My friend and I were staying with her aunt and uncle who were living in Prague on a diplomatic post. We wanted to buy my friend's aunt a thank you gift and couldn't find anything. We finally found a small flower stall and got the saddest-looking bouquet. I remember one store window was just filled with ketchup. We were told it was like that—things would be available in a bulk display one day and then gone the next. We had a small taste of what that felt like on our searches for toilet paper and Clorox wipes during the pandemic, didn't we Doll? Imagine not months, but years of that and what it would do to your emotional and mental state.

Sometimes we have no choice but to triage and operate in survival mode, but we shouldn't underestimate the long-term emotional and spiritual impact it can have, and as I said above, the impact the collective messaging has on our subconscious, and therefore our relationship with money, wealth, and worth.

Well before the pandemic, we were and will continue to be inundated by messages about money and wealth, from advertisers, and storytellers, to the things our parents and grandparents say to our experiences at home and abroad.

We really can't underestimate how a crisis in our finances underpins everything. This is as true for individuals as it is for nations. We also have to appreciate how a crisis in other aspects of our lives impacts our bottom line. Job loss, of course, can quickly turn people's lives upside down and take a devastating financial toll. Health problems are the leading cause of bankruptcies in the U.S.[22] and divorce or separation is also one of the top causes for bankruptcy[23]. The high cost of college continues to make the news as people advocate for mercy on the long-term burden of college loan debt.

The push for college loan forgiveness is a topic that triggers our notions of what is fair, and who is worthy of protection, help, and support. It makes me think of old stories that we have absorbed, like if one group suffered to achieve then every other group must suffer too. Why should they get help and support that I didn't? Versus I wish someone would have helped me to get a leg up. Like the grandfather who told you he walked uphill to school both ways. Who should have access to which resources? That's the deeper question being asked.

We seem to have a knee-jerk reaction to the idea of someone getting something we didn't. If someone gains, we seem to believe someone else loses. And we sure as heck don't want to be the loser. And then to justify this, we tell stories about how one group worked harder, sacrificed more, wasn't wasteful or greedy, and was ultimately more deserving.

The problem with this zero-sum mentality is that it is indicative of a fixed mindset, not a growth mindset. We want a growth mindset in all things, Doll. That means at the macro as well as the micro.

TWO SIDES OF THE SAME COIN

For those that were not financially insecure, the pandemic and sheltering at home provided a quiet time to pull back and spend less. Less eating out. Less grooming. (I said it.) But less discretionary expenditures in general and a brief escape from the rat race. Less keeping up with the Joneses since you couldn't see them. An opportunity to once again, ask. "What is essential to me? Exactly what and how much do I (my family, my kids) need?"

When my husband and I asked ourselves that question, it shifted our lives in the best way. Little did we know how much easier it would make surviving the pandemic and the mini (for us) crisis that was Snowmageddon[24] (others had it much worse.) Three or four years ago we faced a decision to invest in our house that we already struggled to keep up with when it came to normal day-to-day upkeep and larger home maintenance or move. There were lots of big expensive projects looming on the horizon. It wasn't just a financial decision, but a practical decision born out of my chronic health challenges.

Vacuuming and mopping were hard, and it sounds easy to say, "Get a housekeeper," but having someone in the house when I didn't feel well always stressed me out. And I wasn't super happy with the last two people we had, so it felt like a waste of money. (It wasn't necessarily what I wanted to spend money on.) I used a cleaning company for deep cleans and special occasions, but my husband had started helping with the things that were hard for me. And my son helped clean weekly, which was one of the best choices I ever made. I wanted it to be a family effort, but my husband also loved doing the yard. I wished he'd outsource that and free up half a day or more on the weekends. He didn't want to. So, as you can imagine, our weekends were turning into cleaning and chores and keeping up a house that we bought for entertaining, only to have no energy or time left for it. Over time, it started to feel like the house owned us instead of the other way around.

After a particularly rough year of suffering debilitating headaches (a new manifestation of my autoimmune issues) we were at our limit with life. Between the headaches and the medicines, I had been unable to drive my son almost anywhere that year. He was lonely and isolated. We started talking about moving back to our old neighborhood where we had more support, and he could walk or bike to see his friends. We needed life to be easier all the way around.

We had only just started toying with the idea when we decided to check out the market and see what was available, just to get an idea of pricing and what we could get for our money. On our first trip out, we walked into a house and all three of us, plus our dear friend and realtor, immediately fell in love. It was the Goldilocks of our three homes. Our first one began to feel too small and didn't function as well as we needed when we sold, our second home had begun to feel too big and too much, this, our current home, felt just right. All the period charm we loved in our first home plus the entertaining space we loved about our second home, all in a compact, updated, well-appointed package.

We were thrilled. It worked for the three of us but would also be great when our son flew the nest. Not only could he walk and bike and skateboard wherever he wanted to go, on his own, but we were also surrounded by shops and restaurants. We could stop cleaning and maintaining and start living and enjoying again. And rather than be overwhelmed with costly improvements and repairs, our monthly expenses would go down! We couldn't afford to not to buy it.

Two months after we moved in, however, our adventure in downsizing took a not-so-exciting twist. I had killed myself to get us settled and we had just gotten completely unpacked when we discovered a leak in the hall. It took three plumbers to figure out the source and, once we did and filed a claim, our insurance company sent someone out. Well, that day our lives were turned completely upside down.

The news just went from bad to worse. The leak extended throughout our energy-efficient, insulation-filled crawl space. I called my husband at work sobbing. We had to move out immediately. Every lick of furniture, décor, TVs, and the artwork we had just hung on the walls had to be removed. I quickly had to figure out what to keep with us for six to seven weeks and the rest was packed up and put in storage just days later. Like the house was about to be, I was gutted. Our dream house, the solution to all our problems ... not so much.

As the World Turns, so are the *Days of Our Lives.* Life keeps going and finding new and annoying ways to test and try us.

Trying to find a hotel that would accommodate two large dogs was no picnic either. And thanks to our Labrador Houdini, we were kicked out of the first one. We packed all our things that I had once again only just gotten unpacked. Our six to seven weeks turned into five months of hotel living. We wondered what kind of karmic crap was going on. We just couldn't seem to get ahead. Or so it felt.

Fast forward two years to the pandemic—we spent all of it snug as a bug, enjoying the heck out of our backyard and big front porch. Our just-right house has really been just right and even with all three of us home for a year, it worked. It was cozy and comforting and we felt insanely grateful for our outdoor space that was our saving grace. When Snowmageddon, the unprecedented blizzard, that welcomed the new year in Texas hit, we were so glad for the insulation that kept our pipes from freezing.

And now, today, all our goals have been met. We are in a different boat without our big house money pit. We can clean and pull this place together quickly. We have the time and energy to entertain and socialize. I'm gardening more and we can once again ride our bikes to the entertainment district. I admit I sometimes miss our pool, and I had a moment of missing my giant master bedroom when I was quarantined in our tiny bedroom for a month, but other than that there have been few regrets.

When we were displaced between the first and second hotels, I wondered what the message was. What was the lesson in all this? Why was God trying me yet again? To this day I am not sure. Sometimes, the deeper meaning and life lessons are clearer to us than others. Sometimes, you just have to throw your hands up and accept that shit happens. The best I could do at the time was tell myself, *at least we get to model resilience for our son and show him that sometimes you just have to roll with the punches and make the best of it.*

When we peel back the onion, we realize many of the money moves we make are emotionally driven.

Living in a two-bedroom hotel suite with only what you most need was helpful while downsizing and decluttering. All our things are nice, and while I am a more-is-more kind of girl when it comes to decorating and memento keeping, the truth is you don't need a lot. Most of us can comfortably live with much less than we have.

So here we are, in the last chapter, back to the question that started it all, what is essential? How much and what exactly do you want and need? Are what you are paying for and spending your time and money on worth it?

Like much of my adult life, that question was prompted first by my health issues—from a desire to live the best life I could under the circumstances, and to make the most of what I had even when I felt I was lacking much of what I had before. We were stressing ourselves financially in our old house, but that alone wasn't what pushed us to make a decision. It had more to do with feeling like we couldn't keep up and enjoy our life, but the real catalyst was my son feeling stuck alone. It was an emotional decision as much as a financial decision.

When we peel back the onion, we realize many of the money moves we make are emotionally driven. What are your circumstances, Doll? What are you lacking? What are you needing? What desire is pushing you forward to what you need? What emotions are driving your next move?

FINANCIAL AFFAIRS OF THE HEART

In the case of the house, my husband and I felt the same way, shared many of the same emotions, and were aligned in our decisions. The whole thing brought us closer. It was fun having a project to work on together and a new dream to share. But it hadn't always been that way. Financial stress and strain were two things that had been plaguing our marriage for a while—an incredibly common occurrence. Studies show it is the number one cause of arguments in marriage[25]. And, apparently, over half of all marriages start in debt[26]. That wasn't the case for us. When we first married, we were both rocking and rolling, but money still wasn't easy for us to talk about. We were raised very differently on the financial front. I was much more loosey-goosey, and my husband was much more motivated to save and keep a constant and careful accounting of our monthly finances. Thank goodness.

I hated balancing my checkbook. I hated paying my bills. It gave me stress and anxiety even when I had money, so I generally just didn't want to deal with it. And I had always been taken care of and deep down had a sense that everything would work out. But there were some months that would make me nervous if I was being honest with myself.

When we first started talking about getting married, I had some credit card debt. It was such a small amount when I think about it now, but at the time it was probably 10% of my salary so I was starting to sweat it and get stressed. Doug and I were talking about it, and he expressed concern over how I managed (or didn't manage to be more precise) my finances. He couldn't understand how it didn't worry me more and how I could live like that.

179

I remember laying on the couch in my condo and saying, "I don't know, the money just always comes." He was like, "What? What does that even mean?" Then the phone rang. It was my dad. He was calling to let me know that there had been a little money left in the money market he had set up for me for college. It was almost to the dollar the exact amount of my credit card bill! Doug wanted to scream. He could not believe it. He was like, "This is why you are the way you are!"

Those of us who believe in manifesting would say this was proof in the power of my innate sense that money just always comes. Deep down, I believed things would work out, maybe because for me they always had, and I had always had my parents looking out for me and supporting me. But over time, my bad habits did have a way of catching up with me. And I think about the mixed messages I had and put out there around my finances and my money.

I have a friend from college who is one of the hardest workers I have ever known, and he is extremely successful today. One time in my twenties, we were out when I pulled out my wallet to pay for something. I was fumbling to get the right amount because my money was a big fat jumble of wrinkled, crammed-together bills. I can't remember now if he said, "Is that how you handle...?" or "Is that how you keep your money?" But either way, the point is, he was aghast. And that stayed with me. Does the money keep coming if you don't seem to care about it once it's in your wallet?

At that time, I traveled constantly for work. Other staff that worked for me would immediately organize and submit their expense reports as soon as they got back in the office. For me, it was the last thing I tackled, usually right up to the deadline. I felt like I had way more pressing things to handle whenever

I stepped back into the office. I felt like that was prioritizing my needs over the company's needs. I hated organizing all the receipts and dates and tracking down shared expenses. It was annoying busywork. But beneath those behavior patterns and the types of tasks I like or dislike, what else was going on?

Did I feel uncomfortable with the idea of saying, "You owe me this," even when the company literally owed me the money. To this day, I will never ask someone for money they owe me. In fact, a week ago, I organized a gift for someone and didn't want anyone to feel pressured or uncomfortable, so I said just pay what you want, but I didn't purchase the gift based solely on what was collected. I guesstimated and figured I would cover the rest because I wanted it to be a comforting and lovely basket.

I still haven't even added up how much was donated. Why? In this case, it didn't matter. I wanted to give what I wanted to give. So, in addition to believing the money will come, there's several more components to my relationship with money. *I want what I want, I'll figure it out later* and *I don't ever like making people feel uncomfortable* because I assume asking or reminding them that they owe me money will make them feel that way.

When we start to pull it apart, we realize we have many unspoken feelings and rules, and habits when it comes to spending and saving. In my marriage, my feelings of not wanting to deal with managing money came to a head after years of being a stay-at-home mother. The imbalance of me not worrying and my husband being raised to worry and keep a careful accounting and being the one stuck doing it, was further imbalanced by our old-school roles of the husband as breadwinner and wife managing the household. Meaning he earned the money and I spent it. It created a power struggle and a frustrating situation for both of us. And it fed into traditional roles that as a feminist I believed had the potential to be disempowering.

We tried communicating only via email and through spreadsheets because I felt resistant to being managed by my husband. And we finally had to look at both our beliefs and behaviors that were creating resistance. Doug had grown up with parents who were very frugal and saved for retirement. They put off so many things based on this goal of saving for retirement. It was only then that they started traveling the world and splurging more.

Money causes so many problems in relationships because we each have our own relationship with money.

I grew up with the example of my grandparents who had traveled a lot. My grandmother wasn't left with a great deal of savings when my grandfather died, but she was still comfortable. She told me countless times, "Thank goodness we never waited until retirement to travel because your grandfather didn't live long enough to retire." She cherished those memories. And that was the push-pull that Doug and I were having. I didn't want to wait for everything, and prioritize saving above everything else, not just because of some of the experiences and immaturity I described above, but because of my grandparents' experience.

Money causes so many problems in relationships because we each have our own relationship with money. We have our own experiences, stories, and messages that we have internalized. Add to that our unique personalities and values that are also expressed in how we handle money issues. And because money is tied to our most basic, primal needs for food, shelter, and security, we also have a lot of subconscious fears about money. Again, some of which are not even our own but what we absorbed from our parents and grandparents and the financial security we did or didn't experience as children, or they did or didn't experience as children.

Like me believing the money will come, but then not wanting to deal with it when it was there, we often have confusing and conflicting feelings and behaviors when it comes to our finances. Collectively we have been bombarded with mixed messages about money.

- Money can't buy you love.
- You can't have it all.
- We were poor but happy.
- More money, more problems.
- A penny saved is a penny earned.
- No risk, no reward.
- Pull yourself up by your bootstraps.
- Save your money for a rainy day.
- Money is the root of all evil.
- Money makes the world go round.
- Waste not, want not.
- You get what you deserve.
- From rags to riches.
- Money doesn't grow on trees.
- Money talks.
- You have to spend money to make money.

- The best things in life are free.
- You get what you pay for.

YOU OWE IT TO YOURSELF

If we don't get to our core beliefs and shake off the messages that aren't our own or no longer serve us, we're left with a ping-ponging, exhausting relationship with money. Our money can't work for us if we don't know how we want it to work.

Earlier this week, in one 24-hour period, a client and a friend both told me how they splurged on themselves (makeup, facial, skincare, mani-pedi) and felt guilty. They weren't telling me how great they felt or about all the fun they had, instead, they were justifying the expense. I know they are both on a tight budget, but what wasn't clear to me was whether they both think they shouldn't have spent the money, or whether this was just a result of their conditioning about money.

Our money can't work for us if we don't know how we want it to work.

Like the woman who wants the dessert but then complains it will all go to her thighs while she eats the cake.

Was it guilt because their behavior mirrored money habits that caused them problems in the past? Or because they were conditioned to think they shouldn't spend so much on something so frivolous? Or because it was going to add to the debt on the credit card or prevent them from buying something they needed for more practical reasons? Was it more than one thing?

We want things. We need things. After all, we deserve them, Doll. And we really do. Don't we? The problem is that sometimes we want what we don't need. Other times, we aren't in the position to pay for what we most need. More often, we want something we don't need because of another unexpressed need. Sometimes we feel we don't deserve what we want. Or others tell us our material desires are unnecessary, selfish, pretentious, or unattainable. And somehow, we allow their thoughts and beliefs to supersede our own.

When our money messages are muddled, when we get our wants and needs mixed up, when our self-worth isn't aligned with our financial worth, we feel things like buyer's remorse, regret, and shame.

Outside forces are often the catalyst for a financial crisis, but if we are honest with ourselves, our often confusing and faulty relationship with money makes us more susceptible to financial stress and strain. The internal struggle is what has us justifying our purchases and leaves us unclear on if we are repeating old patterns or just still beating ourselves up for past problems with money.

What money messages are going on in your brain, Doll? Now go deeper. What's lurking in the shadows? What is there that shows up as guilt, regret, sneaky behavior, or justification? Hiding shopping bags, pretending you bought something full price, or wearing that dress with the tags on so you can return it?

If you've got your go-to justification on repeat, press pause. Because if you truly believed it, you wouldn't still be ruminating. You wouldn't still be talking it over with your best friend. If you believed you deserved it, or needed it, or were worth it, and knew that it was the truth, you would have moved on, Doll.

Many of us have contributed to self-sabotage by spending when we don't have it, either to keep up with the Joneses or to fill a void. A pile of clothes may have given you a buzz when you were on the shopping spree, but seeing them sitting in the closet can give you the grossest kind of hangover.

And an unmade purchase of something you want can help you uncover the root of that desire and may even be a nudge pushing you in the right direction. Would a house in the neighborhood you covet mean peace and quiet, privacy, or better schools for your kids? Is it pushing you to level up yourself and your goals? Does that BMW you want represent having arrived as an adult? Are you shopping to fill some other void or unexpressed desire?

What are your material desires telling you about your emotional needs and the "you" you'd like to express to the world? The "you" you wish most to be?

Or are your spending habits showing you the parts of your life and yourself that you are avoiding? Are they showing you areas of growth and places where you are devaluing yourself? Are you afraid of what you want? Are you weighing yourself down with debt as a form of self-sabotage? Who and what are you indebted to? What are your decisions costing you?

To be self-actualized, we have to be able to be self-sufficient and stand on our own two feet. That means managing our resources. All of them—our time, our money, our energy. If you aren't a good steward of your money, then what does that imply about how you respect all the other areas of your life?

Only you can determine what is a nicety versus a necessity. Only you can say if what you want is what you need to live your life to the fullest. Only you can decide what makes you feel like you are just surviving and scraping by in life versus really living. You choose how to provide for yourself. You get to name and claim your worth. And you get decide what you keep and what you give away.

What do you need to feel safe, secure, whole? What do you no longer need that would benefit someone else? How can you share the wealth?

Sharing our money, time, and talents increases our mental health and well-being. It doesn't just have to be financial, though monetary donations have been shown to boost happiness[27] Giving of ourselves is also good for our mental health. It increases our self-worth. People who volunteer rate themselves as healthier and more satisfied with their lives.[28]. In helping others, we help ourselves.

Wholeness. Well-being. Health and wealth. Bookends to a rich and fulfilling life. And, as I said before, it all comes down to you. You decide, Doll, when, where, and how to invest your time, energy, talents, and money.

The real bottom line in life is holding yourself accountable to your highest vision of yourself and your life. What is essential and *worth* it to you? Facing the hard stuff in life, the adversity, the challenges, and the painful changes—for all that those trying times may cost us, if we embrace the opportunities to learn more about ourselves, to shift and grow and get back up again, we gain a wiser, stronger, more interesting, and authentic version of ourselves. We owe that to ourselves.

Lessons Learned

♦   If you don't know what you want and how much you need to be content, fulfilled, or happy, you will never have enough.

- Treat your money with the respect you both deserve.
- Less is sometimes more.
- You are allowed to be unapologetic about your desires.
- Recognize your own good fortune.
- Share the wealth—give of your time, talents, and resources.
- Believe in abundance. Life isn't a zero-sum game. Another's loss is not your gain.
- Material comfort matters.
- Forgive yourself and leave your poor choices in the past.
- Know your worth.

Make it a Mantra (Repeat after me, Doll.)

- I am worth it.
- I am fortunate and grateful for all I have.
- My cup runneth over.
- I am living a rich, full life.
- I am safe and secure and can afford to take care of myself and my family.
- I am grateful to be able to give.
- I deserve to be paid well for my experience and expertise.
- Money flows into my life.
- I am investing in myself.
- My choices are in alignment with my financial goals.
- My thoughts and actions create prosperity.
- I believe in abundance. There is always more than enough.
- I manifest riches. I am a money magnet.

- I respect my resources and manage my money with care.
- I am prospering and growing.
- Managing my money brings me peace. Planning for my future gives me security.
- I believe in abundance. There is more than enough for everyone.
- My money works for me. My finances bring me freedom.
- I am not afraid of my finances. I manage my money with confidence.
- My financial discipline pays off in great dividends.

Powerful Questions

- What lessons did you absorb about money while growing up?
- How would you define a rich and prosperous life?
- Are you making decisions that devalue yourself in any way?
- How are you budgeting your time, money, and energy?
- Are you equipped to handle an emergency? Do you have a safety net? Savings?
- What are your most important resources?
- Are you comfortable declaring your worth? If not, what's holding you back?
- What have you earned in life?
- What is it that you can't afford to *not* do?
- What is your deepest material desire? What truth is that propelling you toward?

Journal

Journal

_____

_____

_____

_____

_____

_____

_____

_____

_____

_____

_____

_____

_____

_____

_____

_____

_____

_____

Journal

_____

_____

_____

_____

_____

_____

_____

_____

_____

_____

_____

_____

_____

_____

_____

_____

_____

_____

_____

_____

_____

_____

Epilogue

WALKING IN THE MOONLIGHT

ONE OF MY MANTRAS IS, "I'M WALKING IN THE MOONLIGHT." Whenever I feel afraid, unsure, sad, unclear, or off-track, I repeat it to myself. No matter how lost I am and no matter how dark it gets, I remind myself that I am still walking in the moonlight. There is always light and comfort shining down on me, lighting my way even when I don't know where I am going. Even when everything else is obscured from my knowing, I trust that the moon is there—every night, even all day long. I remind myself that what I need will come, a new day will follow, I just need to keep walking in the moonlight and have faith.

I genuinely believe that we have what we need inside us. But it takes work to find it. It takes work to let ourselves show up fully in all the ways that we need to. And when we can't get to it within ourselves, we will be guided. I believe that the helpers will show up, the teachers will come, the supporters will be there with a shoulder to lean on. But we have to keep moving towards them, walking in faith, putting one foot in front of the other even when it's dark and we're afraid.

I started writing this book both as a gift to myself and as a hurry up and hit your goals because you are now 50! My own midlife crisis if you will. While everything I have experienced has equipped me for where I am today, the journey of writing this book was such a reminder that the learning never ends. And, for me, somehow, that always seems to be expressed through my health. COVID, wouldn't you know, decided to test me and helped to make sure that I could practice what I preach.

When I was close to finishing, when I was down to the last chapter and my first edits, I caught COVID. It had already taken me longer to write with juggling work, family, and volunteer obligations. It felt like a huge setback and after 54 days of fever, it was clear that I was in long-haul COVID territory. I was frustrated, mad, sad, disappointed, and at times, bitter.

I have no idea how I caught it (as is the case for many people). I had done very little, but the few things I had done, I regretted. I succumbed to everything I had written about—that somehow, I actually had control over life and this highly contagious virus. I knew logically that it was surging wildly and was a numbers game, but I kept thinking, "How did I get it, and what could I have done differently?" I was reminded of how hard it is to stay positive when you feel beaten down and are sick and unwell.

COVID is called a novel virus because there is so much that we don't know about it yet, but for me, there was nothing novel about the experience of one more protracted, debilitating, and chronic illness. And that, Doll, was depressing. I saw the pain and struggle others were having in my long-hauler support groups on social media. Many weeks I would log on and someone in one of the groups was suicidal. I was hit with the reminder of just how devastating the loss of health can be—how much not knowing when things would shift can bring us to our knees with fear. I was saddened by the accounts of friends and family who did not believe the profound fatigue and brain fog and myriad symptoms people had many months after their initial illness. I have seen it over and over in one chronic illness group after another. It hurt my heart and weighed on my mind.

It made me more determined to get this book finished as soon as my energy returned. But getting better had me doubling back through all the lessons I have learned and shared with you. I had to let go of work and productivity and give in to rest. My business had been thriving, so sidelining work brought up old pain and fears and deep disappointment.

I had my down days and my fits and starts, and parts of me are still healing. But I got through it just like I have everything else. And I hope that gives my long-hauler, newly minted, chronic illness warriors hope. Things do get better, they do shift, and sometimes the new normal holds blessings in disguise.

Your struggles, your shifts, your changes, and your challenges are creating the next version of your life in ways that may not yet make sense. Do not despair.

I wouldn't choose the life of chronic illness, but it's shaped me into the person I am and given me a perspective I don't know that I could have found any other way. Thank you for letting me share it with you. It is my deepest and humblest hope that this book has been one of your helpers. That you found it at the right time and will come back to it when you need it.

Keep walking in the moonlight, Doll. Keep putting one foot in front of the other. Be your best self. Build your best life. You are the star of your show, and I hope, one of your own heroes. Make it an Emmy-winning performance.

xo Christine

Acknowledgments

I'M BEYOND GRATEFUL FOR THE SUPPORT OF MY FAMILY AND friends. Doug and Patrick, your love and belief in me means everything to me. Thanks for putting up with me when things get hectic, for never giving me a hard time when I have a girls' night, for bringing me drinks and snacks when I am lying in bed, and for loving me as I am.

Special thanks to Doug, Mom, Dad, Nicole, and, especially, Caroline, for being my early readers. Your feedback was thoughtful and important. Dad and Jenn, thank you for helping with the finishing touches.

Thank you to Susie and James for helping me talk through the naming of this book. Thank you to Toni, Lauren, Caroline, and Nicole for listening to me and helping me cope through the process of birthing this baby!

I couldn't have done it without my fur babies, Woodrow and Nicholas (RIP), who give (gave) me unconditional love and unending comfort. You remind me to stretch and play and ask for what I need.

Big thanks, too, to The New Pornographers and Fleetwood Mac. *Challengers* and *Rumours* were on repeat when I was writing.

And, finally, thank you to the angels who watch over me for showing me the signs that I was on the right path.

Two of those angels are my Grandma and Grandpa O'Brien, who always called us "Doll Baby" and "Baby Doll." Every time I typed the word 'Doll', I thought of you and your love. Thank you.

Author Bio

CHRISTINE O'BRIEN HORSTMAN IS THE OWNER OF PAPER Doll Communication. Christine is a Certified Professional Coach with a niche in career coaching. She is also an Accredited DISC Trainer and a Professional Development Instructor. Her wish is that everyone has a life and a career that makes them excited to get out of bed in the morning.

Christine's specialty is emotional intelligence and communication skills. Her real knack is helping people figure out and phrase what they need to say. She helps her clients articulate their worth and what they want.

Christine is a chronic illness warrior who has added long-haul COVID to her resume. Writing has always helped her cope and she believes in the power of putting our thoughts and goals on paper. She honed her writing skills in the *Dallas Morning News*' Community Voices program and was awarded

Most Valuable Contributor. Her poem, "The Long Haul", was published in the Writer's Garret 2021 anthology, *The Common Language Project: Ritual.*

Known for her laugh, Christine brings a healthy dose of humor and playfulness into all that she does and strives to be enthusiastic and engaging whether in her coaching, writing, training, or speaking. She is unable to control her need to call people pet names and terms of endearment, from "Sweetheart", to "Beautiful", to "Doll", of course.

To work with Christine or to have her speak to your group, visit: www.paperdollcommunication.com.

Or connect with her online:

https://www.facebook.com/paperdollcommunication/
https://www.instagram.com/chris.horstman/
https://twitter.com/chronicLYchrisE
Christine (O'Brien) Horstman | LinkedIn

For more information about DISC or to take the assessment:

https://paperdollcommunication.com/coaching/
disc-advantage

Photographer: Rosa Poetschke Photography

Endnotes

1   "Empathy." Lexico. Oxford University Press. https://lexico.com/en/definition/empathy

2   Yu, Christine. "Study Probes the 'Long-Haul' Effects of Covid-19." The Hub, March 22, 2021. https://hub.jhu.edu/2021/03/22/long-covid-long-haulers.

3   "Chronic Diseases in America." Centers for Disease Control and Prevention. Centers for Disease Control and Prevention, January 12, 2021. https://www.cdc.gov/chronicdisease/resources/infographic/chronic-diseases.htm

4   Health, Esther Crain for Women's. "New Study: 1 in 2 People Will Get Cancer." Men's Health. Men's Health, December 5, 2018. https://www.menshealth.com/health/a19536092/1-in-2-people-will-get-cancer.

5   Kagan, Julia. "What Is a Special Needs Child?" Investopedia, January 23, 2021. https://www.investopedia.com/terms/s/specialneedschild.asp

6   "Anxiety in Teens Is Rising: What's Going on?" HealthyChildren.org. Accessed August 4, 2021. https://

www.healthychildren.org/English/health-issues/
conditions/emotional-problems/Pages/Anxiety-
Disorders.aspx.

7   "Any Anxiety Disorder." National Institute of Mental
     Health. U.S. Department of Health and Human Services.
     Accessed August 4, 2021. https://www.nimh.nih.gov/
     health/statistics/any-anxiety-disorder#part_155096.

8   Parker, Kim. "Working-Mom Guilt? Many
     Dads Feel It Too." Pew Research Center. Pew
     Research Center, May 30, 2020. https://www.
     pewresearch.org/fact-tank/2015/04/01/
     working-mom-guilt-many-dads-feel-it-too/.

9   Moore, Anna. "Mother Guilt: Is It Possible to
     Find a Work/Life Balance That Suits Both You
     and Your Children?" For You Magazine. Daily
     Mail Online. Associated Newspapers, October 19,
     2015. https://www.dailymail.co.uk/home/search.
     html?s=&authornamef=Anna+Moore+For+You.

10   Thorsen, Anna. "Dyslexia's Part in the School-to-
     Prison Pipeline: The Inequality Inherent in Our
     Education System." Dyslexia Untied, December
     8, 2019. https://dyslexia-untied.com/2019/10/29/
     dyslexias-part-in-the-school-to-prison-pipeline-the-
     inequality-inherent-in-our-education-system/.

11   "Breaking the School to Prison Pipeline." National
     Council on Disabilities, June 18, 2015. https://ncd.gov/
     publications/2015/06182015

12   "7 Things to Know about the 1 in 5 with Learning
     and Attention Issues." Reading Rockets, May 3, 2021.
     https://www.readingrockets.org/article/7-things-know-
     about-1-5-learning-and-attention-issues.

13 Casselman, Ben. "More than Two Million Workers Have Been without a Job for More than Six Months." The New York Times. The New York Times, October 2, 2020. https://www.nytimes.com/2020/10/02/business/more-than-two-million-workers-have-been-without-a-job-for-more-than-six-months.html#

14 Vozza, Stephanie. "The 'Great Resignation' is Here. This is How Employers Should Prepare." MSN. Fast & Company, June 15, 2021. https://www.msn.com/en-us/lifestyle/career/the-great-resignation-is-here-this-is-how-employers-should-prepare/ar-AAL3XBX#

15 Gogoi, Pallavi. "Stuck-at-Home Moms: The Pandemic's Devastating Toll on Women." NPR. NPR, October 28, 2020. https://www.npr.org/2020/10/28/928253674/stuck-at-home-moms-the-pandemics-devastating-toll-on-women

16 "Maslow's Hierarchy of Needs." Wikipedia. Wikimedia Foundation, August 3, 2021. https://en.wikipedia.org/wiki/Maslow's_hierarchy_of_needs

17 Sorenson, Susan. "How Employee's Strengths Make Your Company Stronger." Gallup.com. Gallup, June 4, 2021. https://news.gallup.com/businessjournal/167462/employees-strengths-company-stronger.aspx.

18 "The Philosophy of IKIGAI: 3 Examples about Finding Purpose." PositivePsychology.com, January 30, 2021. https://positivepsychology.com/ikigai.

19 Harter, Jim and Adkins, Amy. "Employees Want a Lot More from Their Managers." Gallup.com. Gallup, July 9, 2021. https://www.gallup.com/workplace/236570/employees-lot-managers.aspx.

20   "Wealth." Online Etymology Dictionary. https://
       etymonline.com/word/weatlth.
21   "Burgermetister Meisterburger." Fandom.
       Villians Wiki. *"https://villains.fandom.com/wiki/*
       Burgermeister_ Meisterburger
22   Lorie, Konish. "This Is the Real Reason Most Americans
       File for Bankruptcy." CNBC. CNBC, February 11, 2019.
       https://www.cnbc.com/2019/02/11/this-is-the-real-
       reason-most-americans-file-for-bankruptcy.html.
23   Kirkham, Elyssa. "Debt in Marriage: Managing
       Your Finances." LendingTree.com. Lending Tree,
       January 4, 2019. https://www.lendingtree.com/
       debt-consolidation/debt-and-marriage
24   Bogel-Burroughs, Nicholas, McDonnell Nieto del Rio,
       Giulia, and Paybarah, Azi. "Texas Winter Storm: What to
       Know." NYTimes.com. The New York Times, February
       20. 2021. https://www.nytimes.com/2021/02/20/us/
       texas-winter-storm-explainer.html
25   "First Comes Love, Then Comes...Money Trouble?"
       Suntrust.com. Suntrust. https://www.suntrust.com/.../
       article/first-comes-love-then-comes-money-squabbles
26   Kirkham, Elyssa. "Debt in Marriage: Managing
       Your Finances." LendingTree.com. Lending Tree,
       January 4, 2019. https://www.lendingtree.com/
       debt-consolidation/debt-and-marriage
27   Marsh, Jason and Suttie, Julie. "5 Reasons Giving is
       Good for You." Berkley.edu. Greater Good Magazine,
       December 13, 2010. https://greatergood.berkeley.edu/
       article/item/5_ways_giving_is_good_for_you
28   Hopper, Elizabeth. "How Volunteering Can
       Help Your Mental Health." Berkley.edu.

Greater Good Magazine, July 2, 2020. https://greatergood.berkeley.edu/article/item/how_volunteering_can_help_your_mental_health